Scott Foresman - A

MATH

Enrichment Masters
Extend Your Thinking

Grade K

Scott Foresman - Addison Wesley

Editorial Offices: Menlo Park, California • Glenview, Illinois
Sales Offices: Reading, Massachusetts • Atlanta, Georgia • Glenview, Illinois
Carrollton, Texas • Menlo Park, California

http://www.sf.aw.com

ISBN 0–201–31259–X

Copyright © Addison Wesley Longman, Inc.

Printed in the United States of America

6 7 8 9 10 – BW – 02 01 00

Contents

Chapter 9: Time and Money

Chapter 10: Explore Actions with Numbers

Chapter 11: Larger Numbers

Chapter 12: Explore Addition and Subtraction

Overview

Extend Your Thinking *(Enrichment Masters)* enhance student learning by actively involving students in different areas of mathematical reasoning. These masters consist of four types of motivating and challenging activities that focus on higher-order thinking skills. The categories are Patterns, Critical Thinking, Visual Thinking, and Decision Making.

Patterns activities encourage students to develop skills in recognizing patterns that exist in all facets of mathematics. The study of patterns allows students to gain an appreciation for the inter-relatedness and beauty in the structure of mathematics. These activities cover data, numbers, algebra and geometry, and allow students to find interesting solutions to sometimes difficult problems.

Critical Thinking activities challenge students to examine and evaluate their own thinking about math and about related content areas. The strategies students will use include: Classifying and Sorting, Ordering and Sequencing, Using Logic, Drawing Conclusions, Using Number Sense, Making Generalizations, Reasoning with Graphs and Charts, Explaining Reasoning/Justifying Answers, Developing Alternatives, Evaluating Evidence and Conclusions, and Making and Testing Predictions.

Visual Thinking activities focus on students' ability to perceive and mentally manipulate visual images. Emphasis is placed on spatial perception and visual patterns.

Decision Making activities present real-world situations that require students to make a decision. In most cases, there are no clearly right or wrong answers. This gives students the opportunity to carefully weigh alternate courses of action–as well as consider their personal experiences. You may wish to encourage students to use these decision-making steps as they make and evaluate their decisions:

   Understand Encourage students to define the problem. They need to consider why a decision is needed, what goal they wish to meet, and what tools and techniques they can use to reach their decision.

   Plan and Solve Have students identify the information that is relevant to the decision-making process.

   Make a Decision After students evaluate the data and consider the consequences, they decide which choice is best.

   Present the Decision Students explain why they made the choice that they did.

Name _____

Visual Thinking

What do you see?

© Scott Foresman Addison Wesley K

Notes for Home Your child described what he or she saw in the top, middle, and bottom floor of the apartment building. *Home Activity:* Ask your child to tell you on which floor the cat lives. (The top floor)

Name _____

Patterns in Geometry

Draw what comes next.

Notes for Home Your child continued the pattern in each row. *Home Activity:* Ask your child to explain one of the patterns to you.

Name _____

Critical Thinking

Which does not belong?

Notes for Home Your child put an X on the animal that doesn't belong in each group. *Home Activity:* Ask your child to explain his or her choices.

Name _____

Critical Thinking

Match mothers to their babies.

Notes for Home Your child drew lines to match the mother animals to their babies. *Home Activity:* Ask your child to name the animals on the left. (Rabbit, duck, pig, sheep, horse)

4 Use with pages 9–10.

Name _____

Decision Making

Color the animals that make good pets.

© Scott Foresman Addison Wesley **K**

Notes for Home Your child colored the animals that would make good pets. *Home Activity:* Ask your child to explain his or her choices.

Name _____

Patterns in Numbers

Draw what comes next.

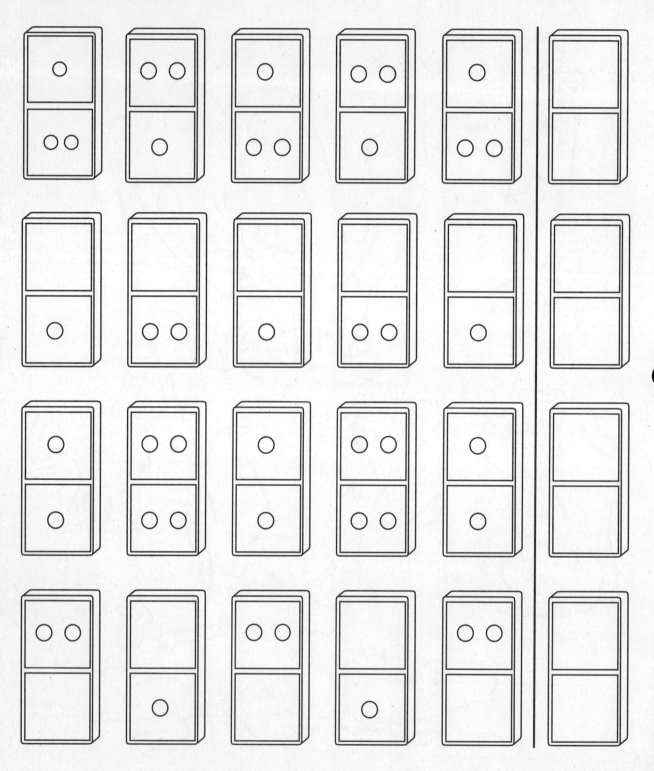

Notes for Home Your child continued the domino pattern in each row. *Home Activity:* Ask your child to choose one row and draw what comes next in the pattern.

Critical Thinking

Color the things.

🖍 green

🖍 orange

🖍 yellow

Notes for Home Your child colored the fruit and vegetables green, the toys orange, and the clothing yellow.
Home Activity: Ask your child to name objects in your home that are green, yellow, or orange.

Decision Making

Match each food to the pan that cooked it.

✂ -

Notes for Home Your child pasted each food to match the pan or tray in which it was cooked. *Home Activity:* Help your child find pans, trays, or other objects in your home that have the same shape as those pictured on the page.

8 Use with pages 17–18.

Name _____

Visual Thinking

Find Rosa's path home.

She only goes , , , and .

© Scott Foresman Addison Wesley **K**

Notes for Home Your child colored each stone with a triangle or a circle on it to make a path home.
Home Activity: Ask your child to tell you about his or her choices.

Name _____

Critical Thinking

What goes together?

Notes for Home Your child drew lines to show the things that go together. *Home Activity:* Ask your child to tell you why the things go together.

Name _____

Visual Thinking

What is missing?

Notes for Home Your child drew what was missing on one animal in each group. *Home Activity:* Ask your child to tell about his or her drawings.

Name _____

Patterns in Numbers

Match the patterns.

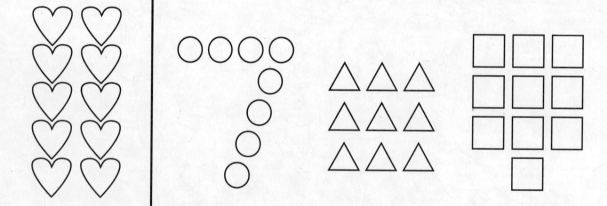

Notes for Home In each row, your child circled the pattern that has the same number of shapes as the pattern at the left. *Home Activity:* Ask your child to explain his or her choices.

Name _____

Visual Thinking

Which path takes less time?

Notes for Home Your child colored the path that takes less time. *Home Activity:* Ask your child to point to the path that takes more time and explain why. (The path on the right would take more time because it has more curves.)

Name _____

Decision Making

What will you pack?

© Scott Foresman Addison Wesley K

Notes for Home Your child colored the things she or he would pack for a trip to a beach. *Home Activity:* Ask your child what he or she could do at the beach.

14 Use with pages 35–36.

Name _____

Decision Making

Collect the objects.

Notes for Home Your child drew lines to match the objects that each child collects. *Home Activity:* Have your child explain his or her choices. Then ask your child to name one more thing that each child could collect.

Patterns in Geometry

Find the patterns.

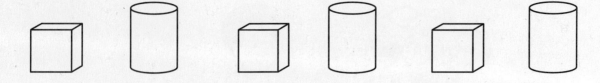

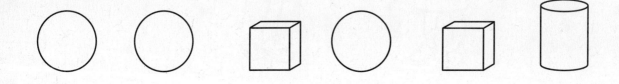

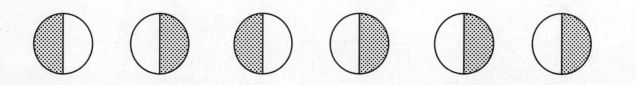

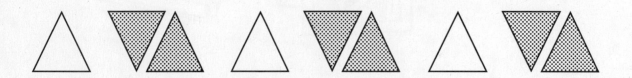

Notes for Home Your child circled each row that shows a pattern of shapes. *Home Activity:* Have your child choose one row that is circled and then draw what would come next in the pattern.

Name _____

Critical Thinking

Make a picture graph.

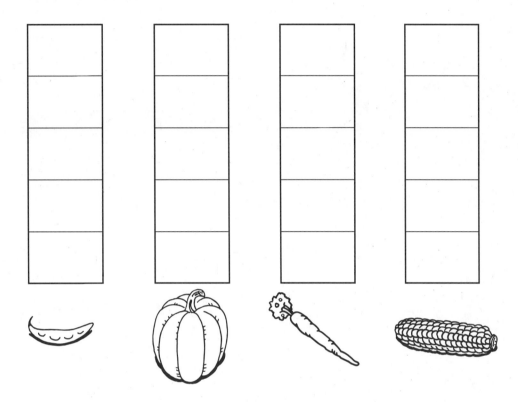

Notes for Home Your child colored a picture graph to show the number of each food. *Home Activity:* Ask your child to tell which food has the most squares colored (string beans), and which food has the least squares colored (pumpkins).

Name _____

Visual Thinking

What's the musical pattern?

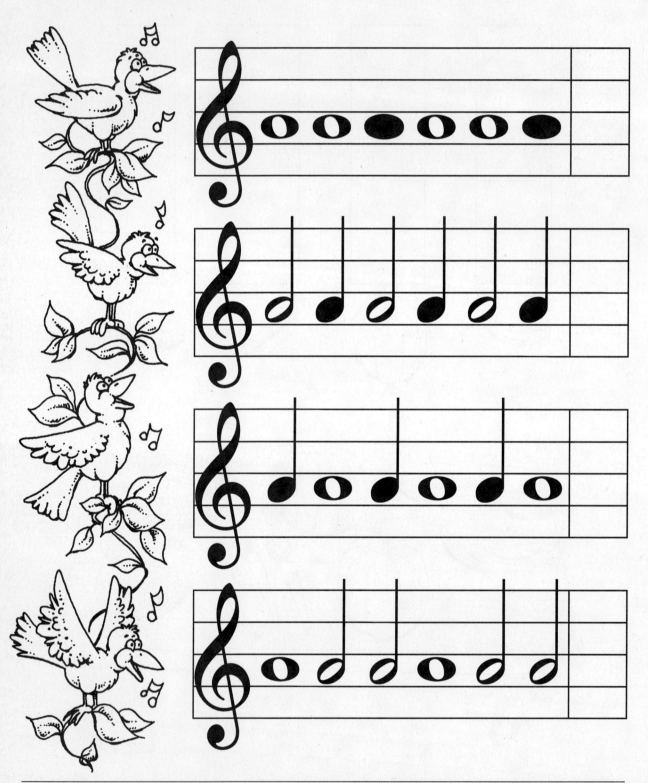

Notes for Home Your child drew the note that comes next in each musical pattern. *Home Activity:* Ask your child to draw his or her own musical pattern below one of the patterns on the page.

Visual Thinking

Which path should each animal take?

 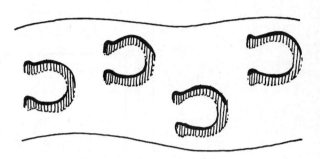

 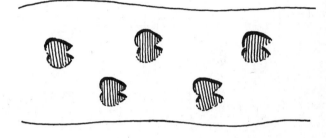

 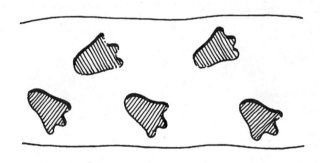

 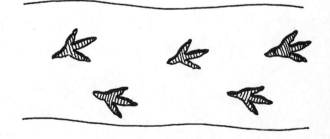

© Scott Foresman Addison Wesley **K**

Notes for Home Your child used picture clues to match the animal to its path. *Home Activity:* Ask your child to explain his or her choices.

Name _____

Decision Making

Match us to our favorite pets.

Notes for Home Your child drew a line to match each child with his or her favorite pet. *Home Activity:* Ask your child to explain his or her choices.

Critical Thinking

What happens next?

© Scott Foresman Addison Wesley **K**

Notes for Home Your child colored the picture that shows what happens next in each row. *Home Activity*: Ask your child to tell what happens first, next and last in each row.

Patterns in Number

Find the pattern.

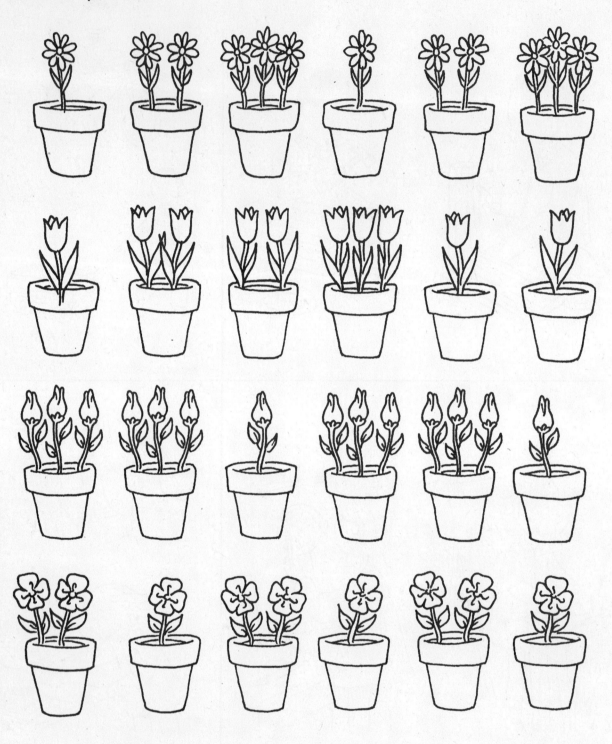

Name _____

Visual Thinking

What's the pattern?

© Scott Foresman Addison Wesley **K**

Notes for Home Your child circled the coin that completed each pattern. *Home Activity:* Give your child 3 pennies and 3 nickels and have him or her make a pattern with the coins.

Name _____

Decision Making

Plan a party.

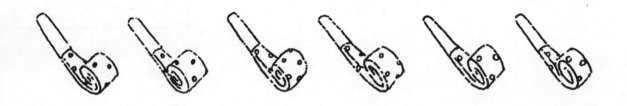

Notes for Home Your child used picture clues to color the items needed for a party. *Home Activity:* Ask your child what else she or he would like to have at the party.

24 Use with pages 61–62.

Critical Thinking

Match the people to the objects.

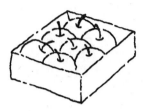

Notes for Home Your child drew lines to match each person pictured on the left to the object he or she would use on his or her job. *Home Activity:* Ask your child to explain his or her choices.

Name _____

Critical Thinking

Color the things that come in pairs.

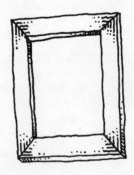

Notes for Home Your child colored the things that come in pairs, or twos. *Home Activity:* Ask your child to name other things that come in pairs, such as slippers and gloves.

Name _____

Extend Your Thinking 4-3

Decision Making

Choose what you and 2 friends would eat for breakfast.

© Scott Foresman Addison Wesley K

Notes for Home Your child made decisions about food items and circled enough breakfast foods for 3 children.
Home Activity: Ask your child to draw a picture of what he or she would eat for breakfast.

Use with pages 73–74. **27**

Critical Thinking

Match the bees to their hives.

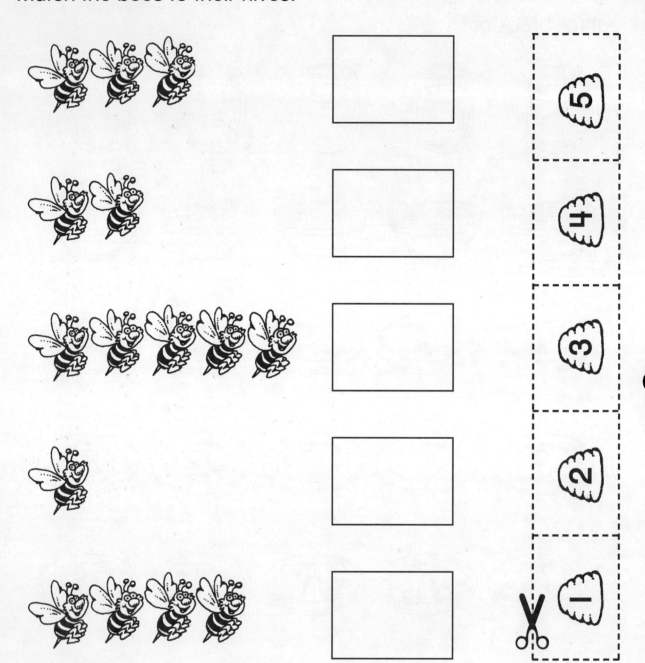

Notes for Home Your child cut and pasted the hives next to the matching number of bees.
Home Activity: Ask your child to point to each number on the page and read it aloud.

Name _____

Visual Thinking

Find the patterns using groups of 3 and 4 beads.

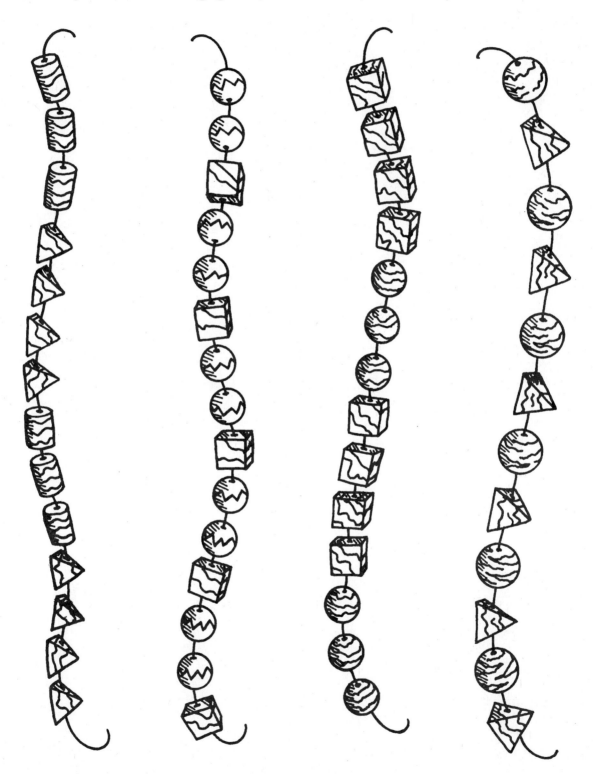

Notes for Home Your child circled the necklaces that have beads in groups of 3 and 4. *Home Activity:* Ask your child to draw a necklace that has a pattern of 3 and 4 beads.

Name _____

Patterns in Numbers

Draw the petals.

Notes for Home Your child identified the patterns shown in the flower petals and then drew the missing petals on the flowers. *Home Activity:* Ask your child to explain the pattern in each flower box. (Box 1: add 1; Box 2: 3, 2, 3, 2; Box 3: 1, 1, 2, 2, 3, 3)

Visual Thinking

How many do you see in each group?

© Scott Foresman Addison Wesley K

Notes for Home Your child identified groups of 0 to 5 and then recorded the number in the table. *Home Activity:* Ask your child to tell how many adults there are in the picture (1) and how many water fountains there are in the picture (1).

Name _____

Critical Thinking

How many wheels are there?

1

3

4

5

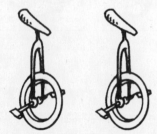

2

Notes for Home Your child drew lines to match the number of wheels shown on the objects in each row to the appropriate number. *Home Activity:* Ask your child to tell how many wheels are on a car (4) and on a wagon (4).

Name _____

Critical Thinking

Write the numbers.

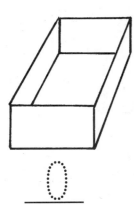

0
_____

_____

_____

_____

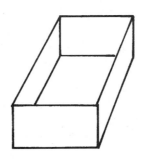

_____

_____

_____

_____

_____

Notes for Home Your child counted the objects in each box and wrote the appropriate number on the line.
Home Activity: Ask your child to circle the empty boxes.

Name _____

Patterns in Geometry

Draw what comes next in each row.

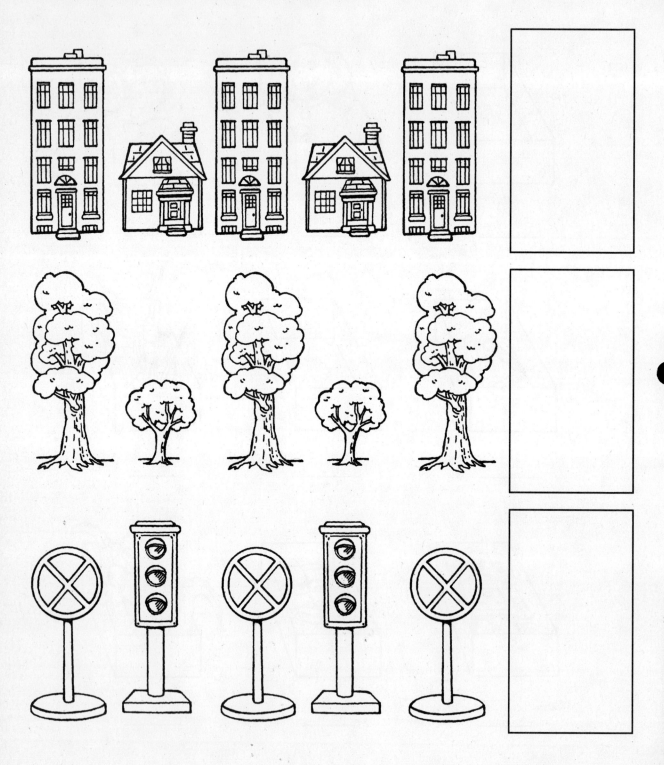

Notes for Home Your child drew what comes next in each row. *Home Activity:* Ask your child to draw his or her own pattern.

Name _____

Decision Making

Which will you build?

What will you use?

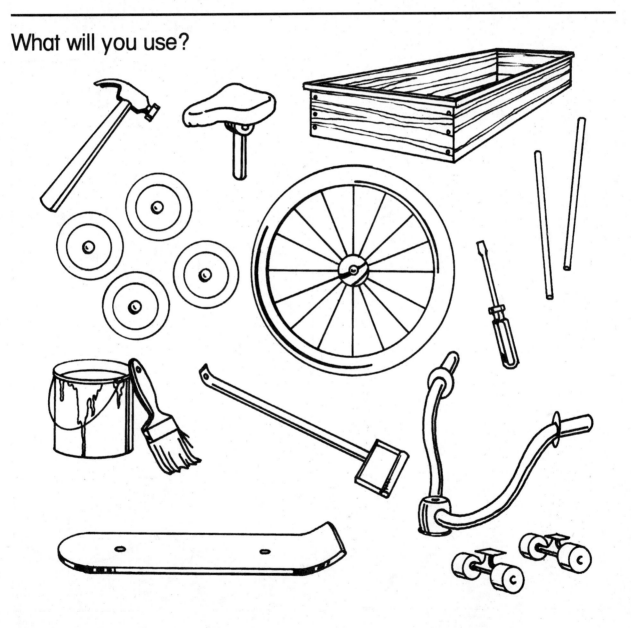

Notes for Home Your child decided what he or she would build and circled that object. Then your child colored the things that he or she would use to build the object. *Home Activity:* Have your child explain how he or she would build the object in sequential order.

Name _____

Visual Thinking

Find the numbers and color.

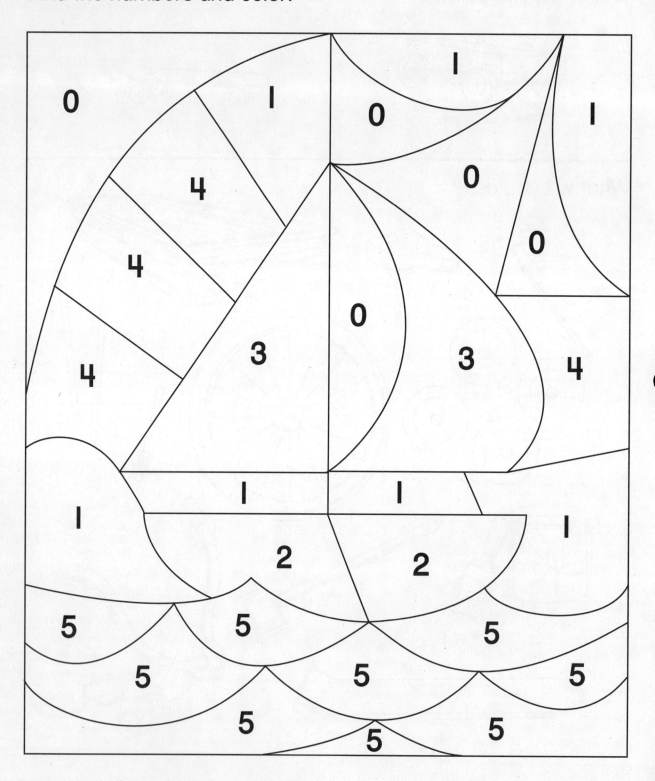

Notes for Home Your child identified the numbers 2 and 3. Then he or she colored the 3s yellow and the 2s red.
Home Activity: Have your child color the 5s blue.

36 Use with pages 91–92.

© Scott Foresman Addison Wesley K

Name _____

Critical Thinking

Circle the object that does not belong.

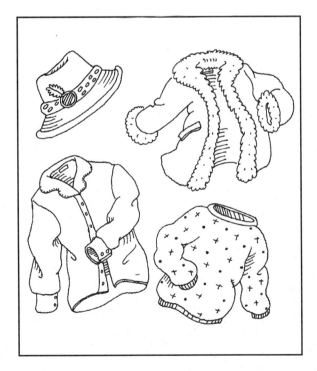

Notes for Home Your child circled the object that does not belong in each group. *Home Activity:* Have your child explain his or her answers.

Name _____

Visual Thinking

Put the animals in their homes.

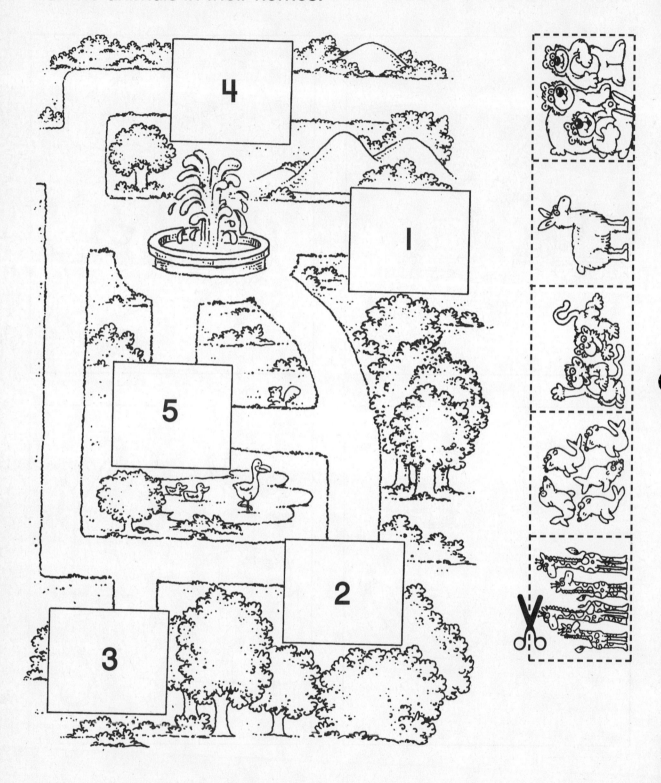

Notes for Home Your child cut and pasted the animals where they belong in the zoo by matching the animals to the appropriate numbers. *Home Activity:* Have your child count to 5 in order.

Visual Thinking

Count the objects.

© Scott Foresman Addison Wesley **K**

Notes for Home Your child identified objects and counted them. Then he or she wrote the numbers in a table.
Home Activity: Ask your child if there are more cans or more balls. (cans)

Critical Thinking

Match the clowns to dots on their ties.

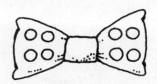

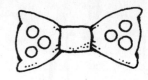

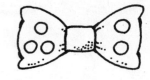

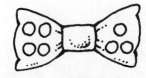

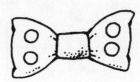

Notes for Home Your child identified the number on each clown and then drew lines to match each clown with the tie that has that number of dots. *Home Activity:* Ask your child to count in order from 1 to 8.

Name _____

Patterns in Number

Draw what is missing.

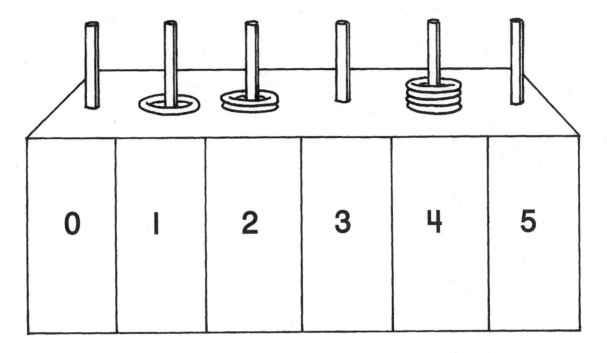

| 0 | 1 | 2 | 3 | 4 | 5 |

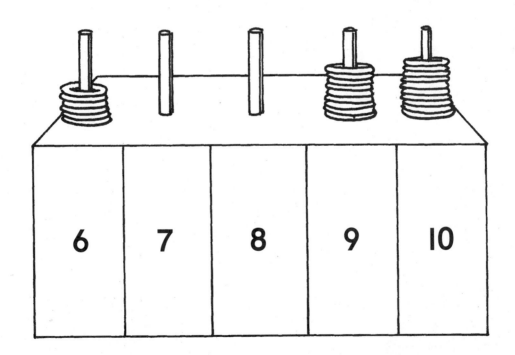

| 6 | 7 | 8 | 9 | 10 |

Notes for Home Your child drew the missing rings to complete the pattern. *Home Activity:* Ask your child to count in order from 0 to 10 as you point to each number.

Name _____

Critical Thinking

Write the numbers.

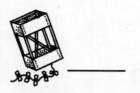 _____

 _____

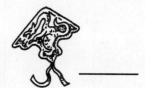 _____

 _____

 _____

Notes for Home Your child decided how many of each kind of kite is shown in the pictograph and then wrote the number. *Home Activity:* Ask your child to explain which kite was his or her favorite.

Name _____

Decision Making

Circle 5 toys.

Notes for Home Your child chose 5 toys and wrote their numbers in order. *Home Activity:* Ask your child to recite the numbers 1 to 10 in order.

Name _____

Visual Thinking

Draw objects.

Extend Your Thinking
5-8

Notes for Home Your child drew 1 house with 4 windows, 2 trees, 5 birds, and 8 flowers. *Home Activity:* Ask your child to draw 3 bikes in front of the house.

44 Use with pages 113–114.

© Scott Foresman Addison Wesley K

Name _____

Critical Thinking

Who is the strongest?

Notes for Home Your child counted the shaded boxes on each scale and wrote the number to tell who was the strongest. Then he or she circled the strongest clown by determining which clown has the most shaded boxes. *Home Activity:* Ask your child to put an X on the weakest clown and explain his or her choice.

Visual Thinking

Connect the dots.

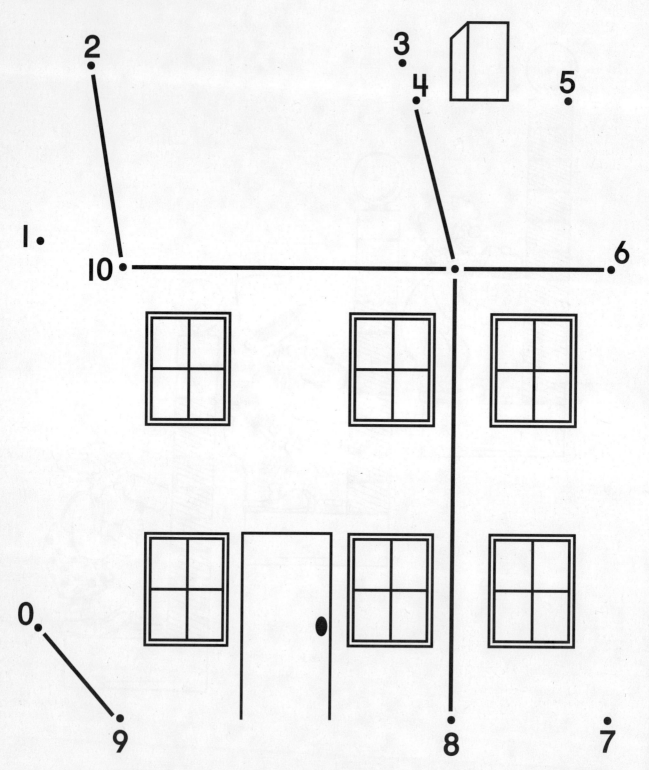

Notes for Home Your child connected the dots in order to make a picture. *Home Activity:* Ask your child to count back from 10 in order, as you point to each number.

46 Use with pages 117–118.

Patterns in Geometry

Find the patterns.

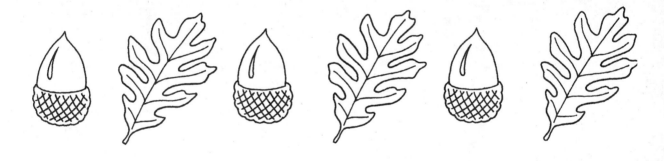

Notes for Home Your child circled the rows that show a pattern. *Home Activity:* Ask your child to choose one of the rows he or she circled and tell what would be the next 2 objects in that row. (Row 3: acorn and leaf; Row 4: maple leaf and elm leaf)

Decision Making

What would you use?

Notes for Home Your child looked at each scene and then colored the object that would be most useful in that situation. *Home Activity:* Ask your child to name at least one other thing he or she would use in each situation, such as a raincoat on a rainy day.

Name _____

Visual Thinking

Match the sets.

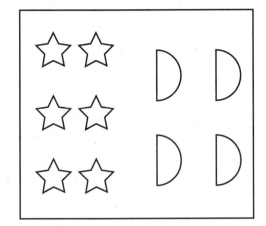

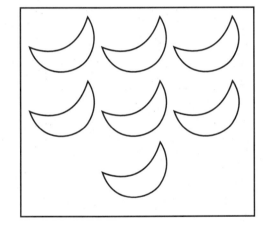

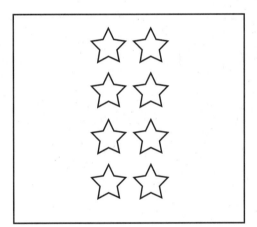

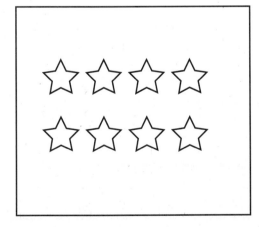

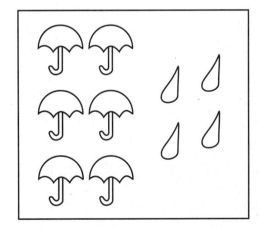

© Scott Foresman Addison Wesley K

Notes for Home Your child drew lines to match the number of objects in the sets. *Home Activity:* Have your child explain his or her reasoning.

Use with pages 123–124. **49**

Name _____

Critical Thinking

Match.

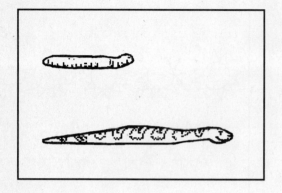

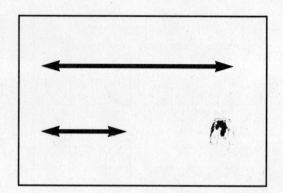

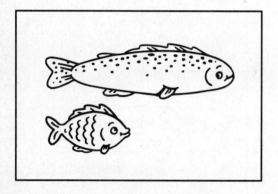

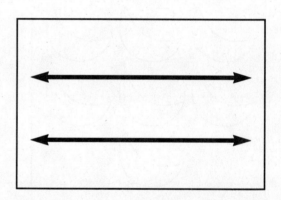

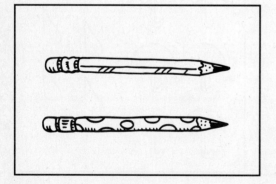

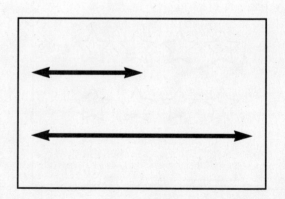

Notes for Home Your child compared the length of objects and drew lines from pairs of real objects to lines that match their proportions. *Home Activity:* Ask your child to compare the length of 2 household objects, such as a fork and a teaspoon.

Name _____

Visual Thinking

How long are these things?

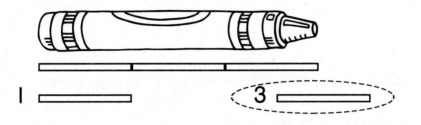

1 ▭   3 ⬭   5 ▭

2 ▭   3 ▭   4 ▭

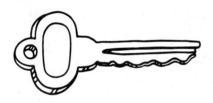

2 ▭   3 ▭   4 ▭

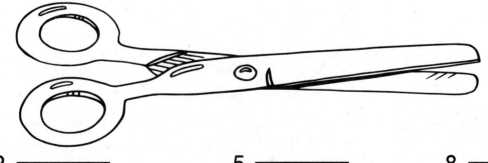

2 ▭   5 ▭   8 ▭

© Scott Foresman Addison Wesley K

Notes for Home Your child estimated the length of objects and circled the closest estimate. *Home Activity:* Ask your child to estimate how long his or her finger is using the shape on this page.

Name _____

Decision Making

Which one will you use?

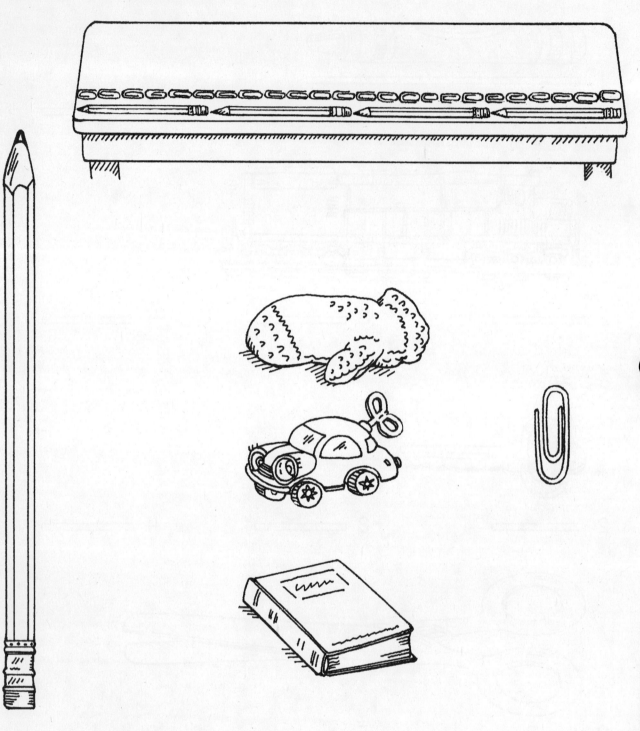

Notes for Home Your child drew lines to show which nonstandard unit of measure (a paper clip or a pencil) he or she would use to find the length of the actual objects. *Home Activity:* Have your child use a teaspoon to measure the length of the kitchen table. Ask your child: *How many teaspoons wide is the table?*

Name _____

Name _____

Patterns

Finish each pattern.

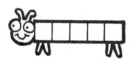  

   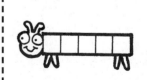

Notes for Home Your child cut and pasted the next item in each pattern. *Home Activity:* Ask your child to draw a picture to extend one of the first three patterns.

Decision Making

Which one would you use?

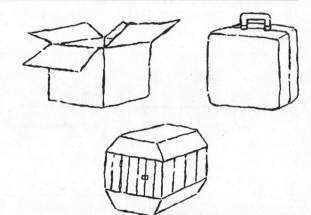

Notes for Home Your child compared the capacity of different containers and chose the one he or she considered most appropriate for a given task. *Home Activity:* Ask your child to explain his or her reasoning.

Name _____

Visual Thinking

Draw lines to match.

© Scott Foresman Addison Wesley K

Notes for Home Your child drew lines connecting soup tureens of different sizes to the groups of small bowls that could be filled from each. *Home Activity:* Ask your child to estimate how many water glasses can be filled from a pitcher and then help him or her test the guess.

Critical Thinking

Which one is lightest?

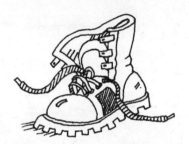

Notes for Home Your child compared the weights of objects, circling the object in each row that weighs the least. *Home Activity:* Ask your child to guess which member of your family weighs the least. Then check his or her guess by weighing all family members and comparing their weights.

Name _____

Visual Thinking

Draw a line to the right group.

heavy

light

Notes for Home Your child estimated the weight of animals and grouped them as heavy or light. *Home Activity:* Ask your child to guess which animal is heavier—a squirrel or an eagle—and then together look up their weights in an encyclopedia to find the answer.

Name _____

Patterns

Circle the patterns.

Notes for Home Your child identified and circled patterns involving shapes. *Home Activity:* Ask your child what he or she would change in the second row of shapes to make a pattern. (Possible answer: change the last small square into a large square.)

Name _____

Visual Thinking

Which are boxes, cylinders, or balls?

Notes for Home Your child identified rectangular prisms or boxes, cylinders, and spheres or balls. He or she drew an X on each box, colored the cylinders, and circled the spheres. *Home Activity:* Ask your child to draw spots on the cones in the picture.

Name _____

Patterns in Geometry

What comes next?

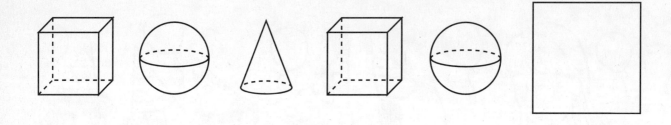

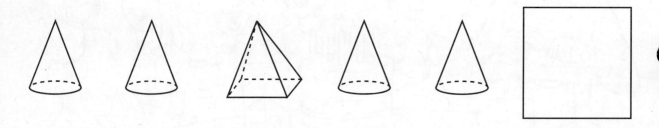

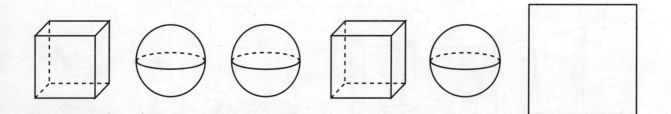

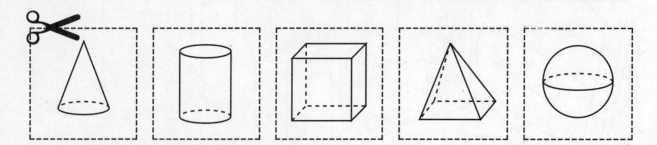

Notes for Home Your child identified and continued patterns involving shapes. *Home Activity:* Ask your child to explain one of the patterns to you and tell what shape should come next.

Name _____

Critical Thinking

Which hole will each shape go through?

 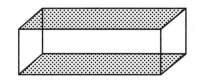 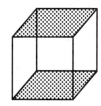

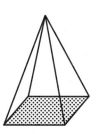 

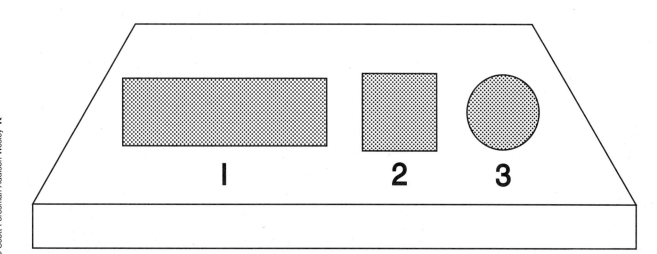

1   2   3

© Scott Foresman Addison Wesley **K**

Notes for Home Your child matched the shape of one face of each solid—a cone, 2 rectangular prisms, a pyramid, a cylinder, and a sphere—with a figure of the same shape. *Home Activity:* Ask your child to describe or draw the hole that the pyramid would go through if it were turned sideways.

Critical Thinking

Which one does not belong?

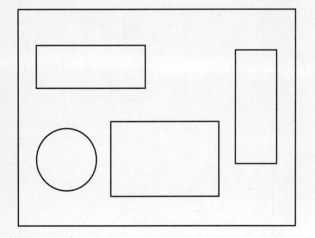
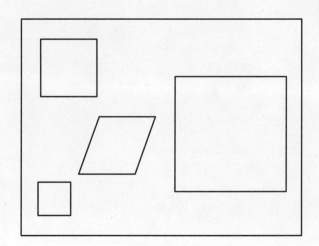

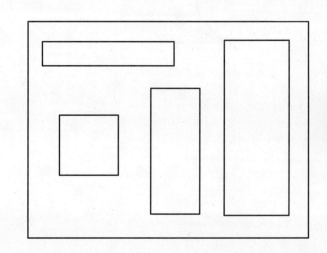

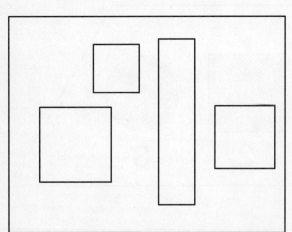
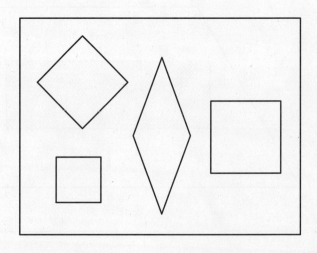

Notes for Home Your child identified the shape that does not share the attributes of the other shapes in its group, crossing off the one that is different. *Home Activity:* Ask your child to identify 3 of the crossed-out shapes that could be grouped together, and to tell what attribute(s) they have in common.

Name _____

Patterns in Geometry

Draw what comes next.

Notes for Home Your child identified and continued patterns involving shapes. *Home Activity:* Ask your child to make up an original pattern and to draw the first 5 or 6 shapes in it.

Decision Making

Draw the shapes to make your own pictures.

Add 4 △ .

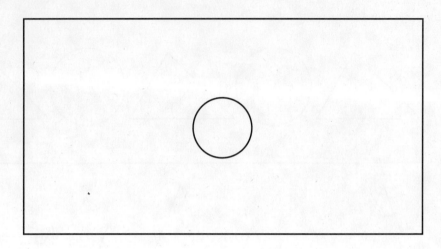

Add 4 △
and 2 ▭ .

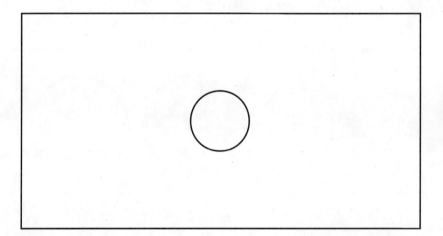

Add 4 △
and 2 ▭
and 1 ▢ .

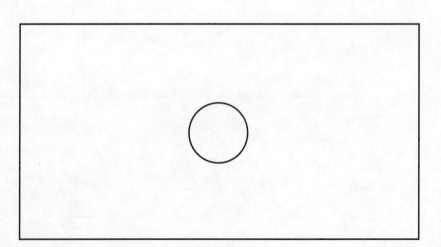

Notes for Home Your child drew an assigned number of triangles, rectangles, and squares to compose designs made of shapes. *Home Activity:* Ask your child to describe and compare his or her 3 designs.

© Scott Foresman Addison Wesley **K**

Name _____

Visual Thinking
Color the shapes.

Notes for Home Your child colored the triangles yellow, the rectangles red, and the circles blue. *Home Activity:* Ask your child to draw a picture without using triangles, rectangles, or circles.

Name _____

Patterns

Circle patterns.

Notes for Home Your child circled rows with repeating patterns. *Home Activity:* Ask your child to identify the next 3 objects in the pattern in row 4. (fish, turtle, snail)

Critical Thinking

Draw lines to match.

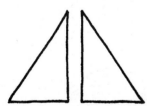

Notes for Home Your child matched objects that were divided into 2 parts and those that were whole.
Home Activity: Ask your child to draw pictures of whole objects and divide them into 2 equal parts.

Name _____

Decision Making

Draw lines to share.

Notes for Home Your child separated several pairs of items into 2 equal groups. *Home Activity:* Ask your child to draw 2 apples on the page and show how they could be shared equally.

Name _____

Visual Thinking

Color the triangles.

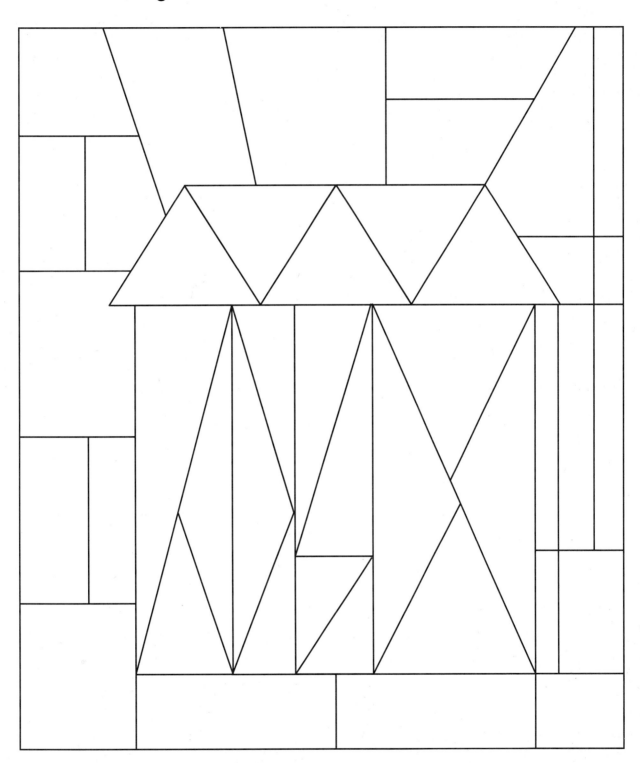

Notes for Home Your child colored triangles to find a hidden picture. *Home Activity:* Ask your child to count the triangles in the roof that he or she colored. (There are 5 triangles.)

Name ______________________________

Extend Your Thinking 8-1

Decision Making

Choose a fruit for each box. Draw the right number.

3

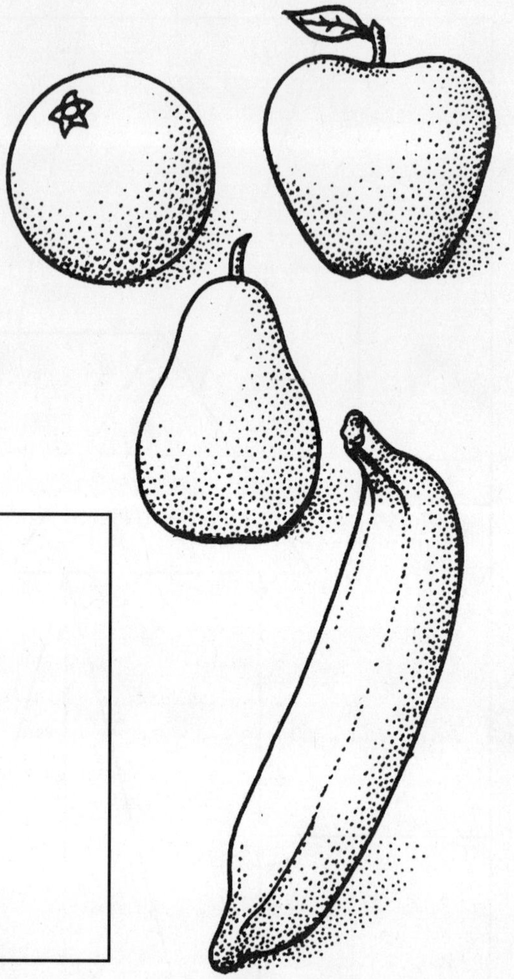

5

7

Notes for Home Your child chose fruits and drew them the correct number of times to illustrate 3 numbers.
Home Activity: Ask your child to choose a fruit and draw it enough times to illustrate the number 4.

Name _____

Visual Thinking

Trace the path marked by groups of 4 birds.

© Scott Foresman Addison Wesley K

Notes for Home Your child identified groups of 4 birds and followed them to find the way through a maze.
Home Activity: Ask your child to point out at least 3 pieces of furniture with 4 legs each.

Name _____

Critical Thinking

Circle each tile with 6 dots in all.

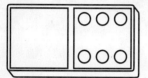 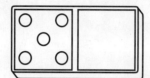 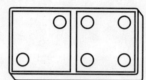 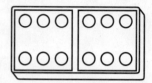

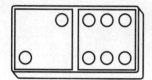 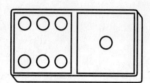 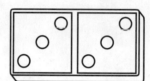 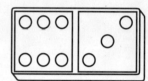

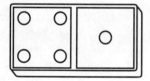 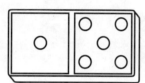 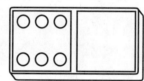 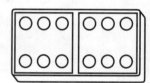

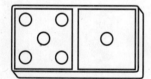 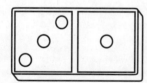 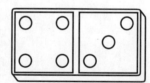 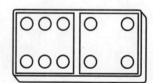

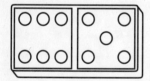 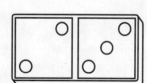 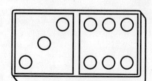 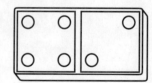

Notes for Home Your child identified domino tiles that showed 6 dots in all. *Home Activity:* Ask your child to list aloud all the combinations circled on this page that have the sum of 6.

Patterns

What comes next?

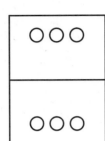 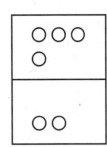 

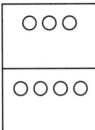 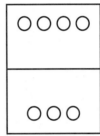 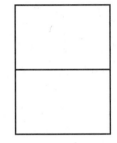

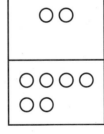 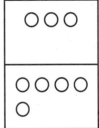

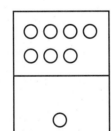 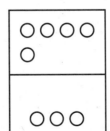

Notes for Home Your child recognized patterns involving grouping 6 dots, 7 dots, and 8 dots, and continued each pattern. *Home Activity:* Ask your child to explain one of the patterns to you and continue it one more step.

Visual Thinking

Connect each pair of groups that make 10.

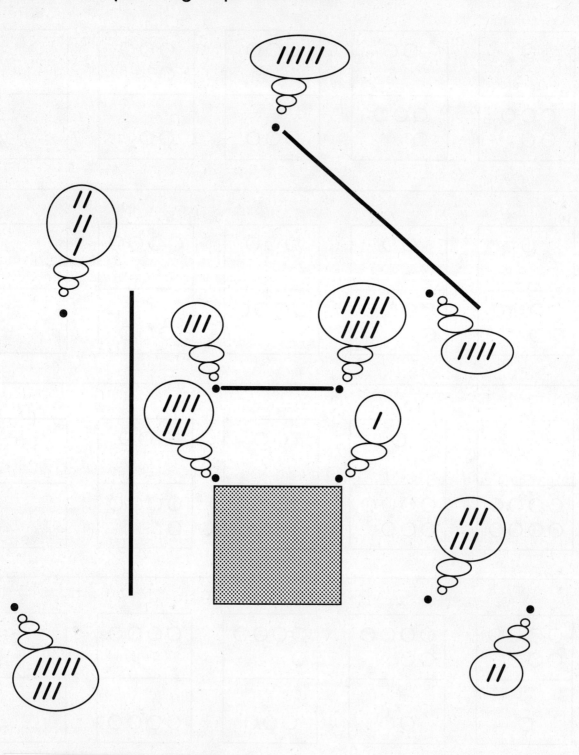

© Scott Foresman Addison Wesley K

Notes for Home Your child drew lines to match groups of tally marks that, together, total 10. *Home Activity:* Ask your child to make up an appropriate address for this house.

Critical Thinking

Count and match.

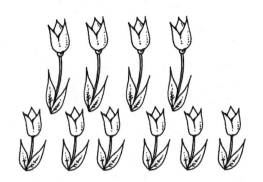

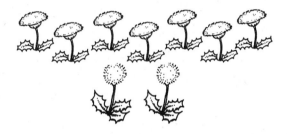

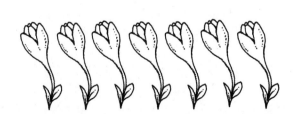

Notes for Home Your child identified the total number of items in each of 8 groups, and drew lines to match groups with the same totals. *Home Activity:* Ask your child to tell how many would be in each group at the left of the page if one more flower were added to each set.

Name _____

Decision Making

Match each box with any number.
Color that many.

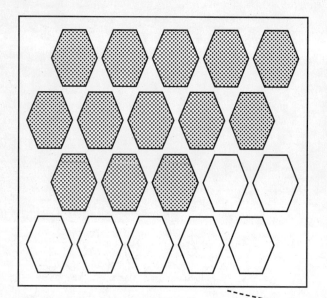 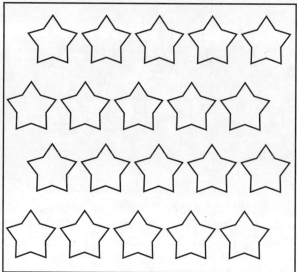

15   18   12   17   13   19

Notes for Home Your child selected the number of objects to be colored in each box, drew lines to connect the numbers with the boxes, and colored the number of objects chosen. *Home Activity:* Ask your child to choose one of the remaining numbers and draw that many circles on a paper.

Critical Thinking

How much does each weigh?

1 pound

5 pounds

10 pounds

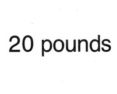

20 pounds

© Scott Foresman Addison Wesley K

Notes for Home Your child matched animals with their approximate weights, between 1 and 20 pounds.
Home Activity: Help your child to weigh himself or herself and compare that weight with those of the animals pictured.

Name _____

Visual Thinking

How long is each thing?

_____ inches

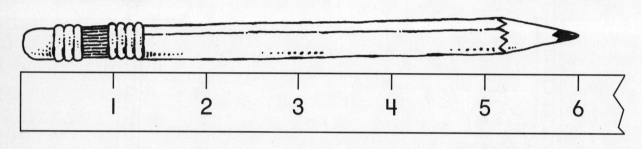

_____ inches

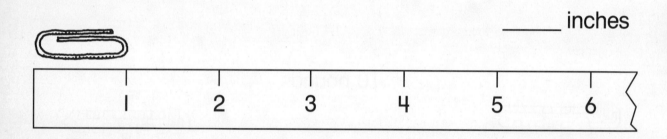

_____ inches

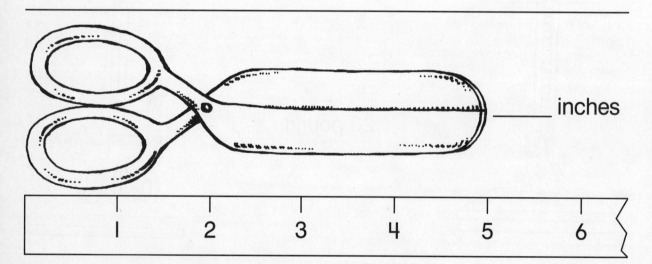

Notes for Home Your child compared objects to full-size illustrations of rulers to find their lengths. *Home Activity:* Ask your child to decide whether each of these things is longer or shorter than 6 inches: a cracker, a man's shoe, a person's thumb.

© Scott Foresman Addison Wesley K

Name _____

Patterns

What comes next?

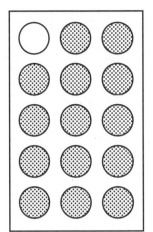 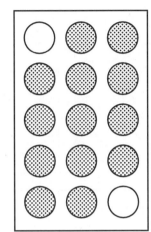 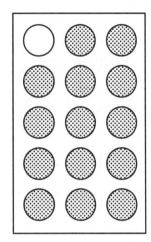 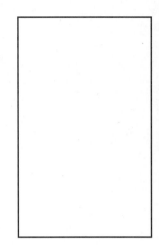

 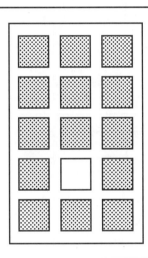 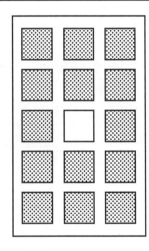 

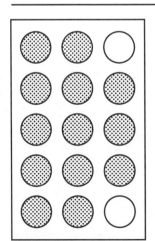 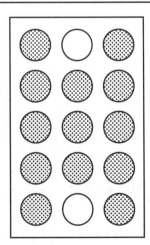 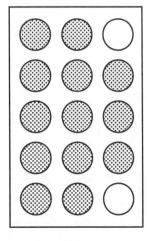 

Notes for Home Your child identified and continued 3 patterns. *Home Activity:* Ask your child to explain each of the patterns to you.

Name _____

Critical Thinking

What comes before or after?

Notes for Home Your child identified events that come before and after given events. *Home Activity:* Ask your child to explain what is happening in each of the pictures.

Name _____

Patterns

What comes next?

Notes for Home Your child identified the next event in a repeating pattern of events. *Home Activity:* Ask your child to dramatize one of the exercises pictured on this page.

Name _____

Visual Thinking

Cross out the clocks that are wrong.

Notes for Home Your child identified clocks whose numerals were incorrect or missing. *Home Activity:* Ask your child to explain what was wrong with each of the clocks he or she crossed out.

Name _____

Decision Making

What time would you do this?

Notes for Home Your child read clocks to the hour and circled preferred times for given activities. *Home Activity:* Ask your child to explain his or her choices.

Name _____

Critical Thinking

What comes before the party?

Notes for Home Your child circled events that usually happen before a birthday party. *Home Activity:* Ask your child to think of events that happen during and after a birthday party.

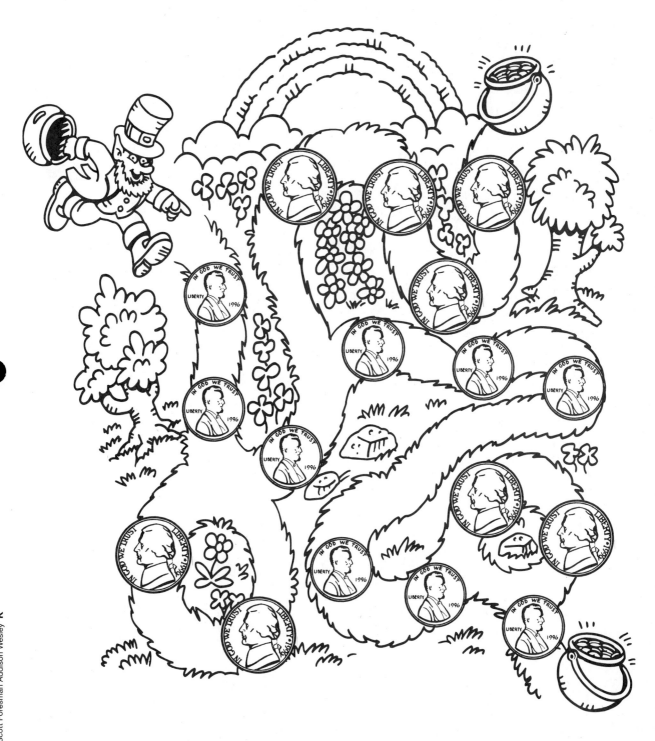

Visual Thinking

Draw a line to find the pennies.

Name _____

Decision Making

Choose 2 things to buy with

these coins: .

5¢

4¢

Notes for Home Your child found the value of a set of coins and circled 2 items he or she could buy with 9 cents. *Home Activity:* Ask your child to tell how many cents would be left over if he or she chose 2 items from the 4¢ shelf. (1¢)

86 Use with pages 221–222.

Patterns

What comes next?

     |

   |

    |

© Scott Foresman Addison Wesley K

Notes for Home Your child calculated the value of coin combinations in patterns and drew a line to the coin combination that extends each pattern of values. *Home Activity:* Ask your child to extend the second pattern by one more coin combination. (2 dimes)

Name _____

Critical Thinking

Which ones can I buy?

12¢

25¢

18¢

15¢

10¢

20¢

Notes for Home Your child decided the value of a coin combination and circled items that cost that amount or less. *Home Activity:* Ask your child to choose one thing he or she would buy with the given amount of money and the same choices of items.

88 Use with pages 225–226.

Name _____

Visual Thinking

Cross out the gift that is wrong for each one.

Notes for Home Your child crossed out the gift that was not appropriate. *Home Activity:* Ask your child to explain his or her choices.

Name _____

Visual Thinking

Circle how many are coming.

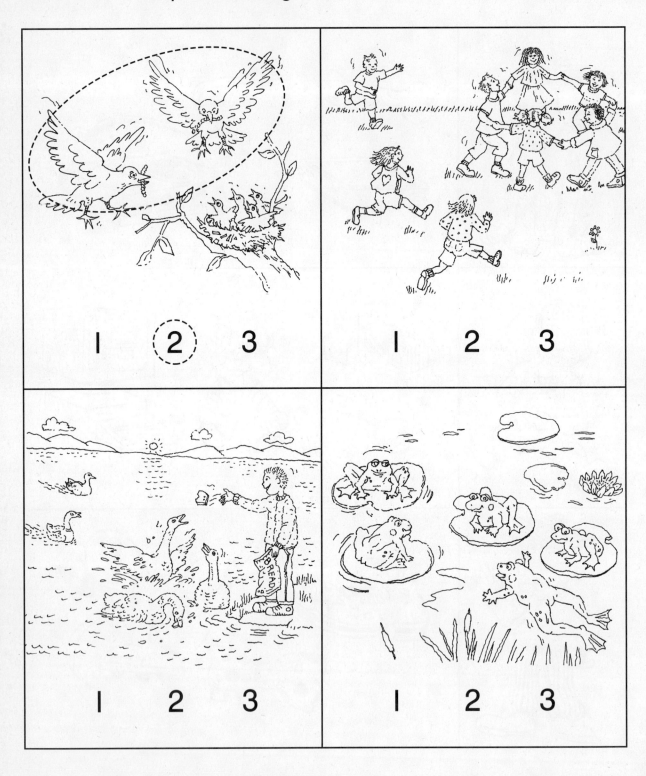

Notes for Home Your child circled people or animals and the numbers to show how many are coming.
Home Activity: Ask your child to tell a joining story about each picture.

90 Use with pages 235–236.

Decision Making

Draw how many you want.

Notes for Home Your child drew more items to be added to a given number of items. *Home Activity:* Ask your child to draw a picture of a favorite toy and then draw a picture of how many more he or she would like to own.

Name _____

Critical Thinking

Circle how many are left.

5   4   (2)

3   2   4

1   3   2

3   2   4

Notes for Home Your child compared pictures and circled the number of items left in the second picture.
Home Activity: Ask your child to tell a number story about each pair of pictures.

Decision Making

How much goes to the first animal?

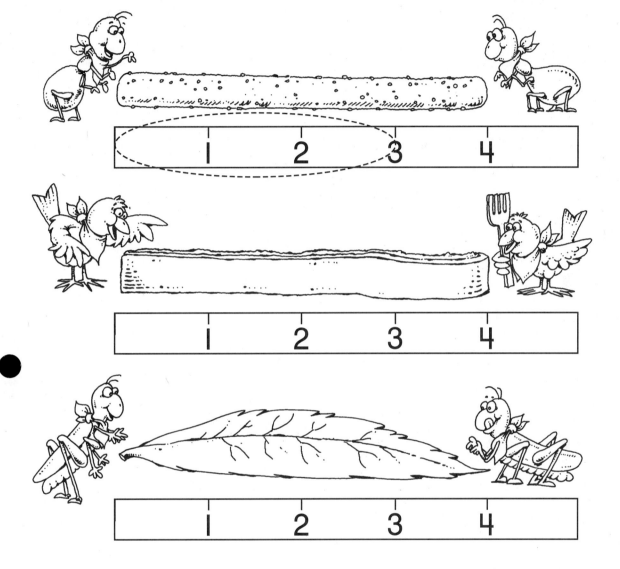

Notes for Home Your child circled how much of a food item should go to the first hungry animal. *Home Activity:* Ask your child to cover the part of the food item circled for the first animal and count the units of food left for the second animal.

Name _____

Patterns in Numbers

Circle the number that is missing.

1 2 ___ 4 5	3 6
3 4 5 ___ 7	8 6
2 4 6 8 ___	10 9
5 4 3 ___ 1	6 2
1 3 5 ___ 9	6 7
10 9 8 ___ 6	7 4

© Scott Foresman Addison Wesley K

Notes for Home Your child completed number patterns. *Home Activity:* Ask your child to explain his or her reasoning.

Name _____

Critical Thinking

Cross off the ones that are not equal.

© Scott Foresman Addison Wesley K

Notes for Home Your child compared the number of objects in pairs of groups and crossed out the pairs with unequal numbers of objects. *Home Activity:* For each box, ask your child to tell which group of objects has more.

Name _____

Visual Thinking

Circle the longer object.

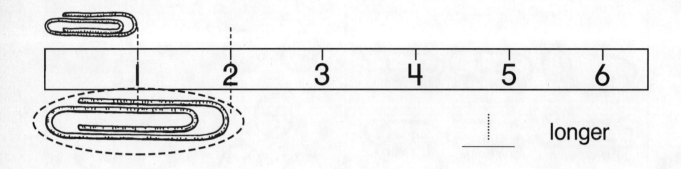

2   3   4   5   6

____ longer

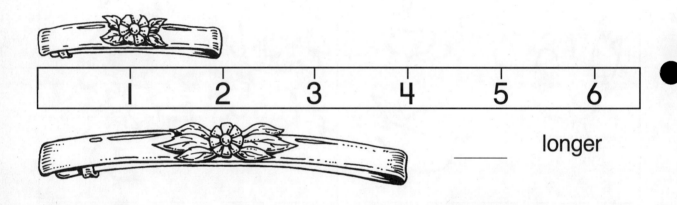

1   2   3   4   5   6

____ longer

1   2   3   4   5   6

____ shorter

Notes for Home Your child compared the lengths of 2 objects, drew a line to each object's length, and circled the longer object. *Home Activity:* Ask your child to measure 2 small objects, using the ruler on this page or another ruler, and tell which object is longer.

Name _____

Patterns

What comes next?

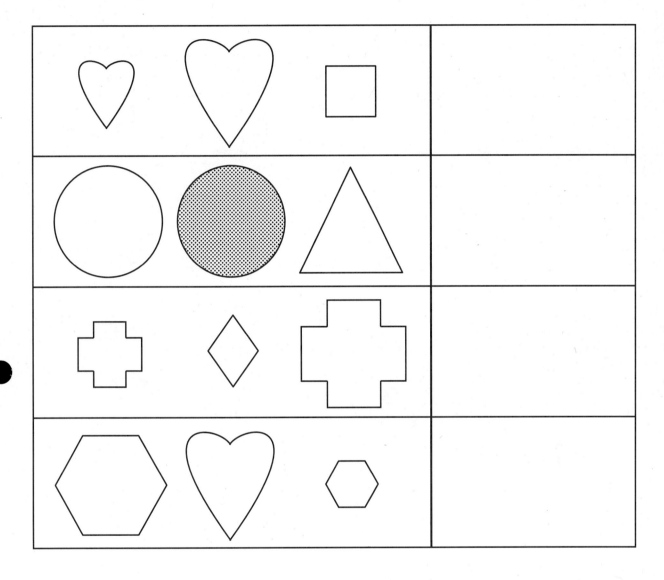

Notes for Home Your child completed each pattern by cutting and pasting the missing item. *Home Activity:* Ask your child to explain his or her reasoning.

Name _____

Critical Thinking

Count. Circle the correct numbers.

29   30   31

14   16   17

23   24   26

Notes for Home Your child counted groups to 30 and circled the correct totals. *Home Activity:* Ask your child to show with his or her fingers how to count, by ones, to 30.

Name _____

Patterns in Numbers

What comes next?

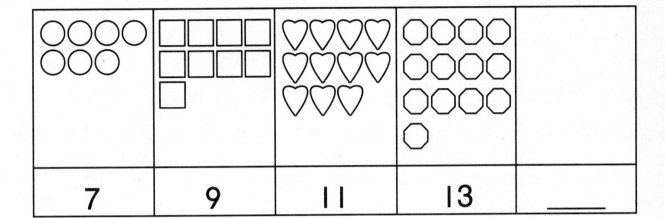

| 7 | 9 | 11 | 13 | _____ |

| 2 | 5 | 8 | 11 | _____ |

| 1 | 11 | 2 | 12 | 3 | _____ |

Notes for Home Your child identified patterns in numbers and then continued each pattern. *Home Activity:* Ask your child to explain each of the patterns to you. (First row: +2; second row: +3; third row: +10.)

Name _____

Visual Thinking

Color by numbers.

16—orange   17—blue   18—yellow   19—green

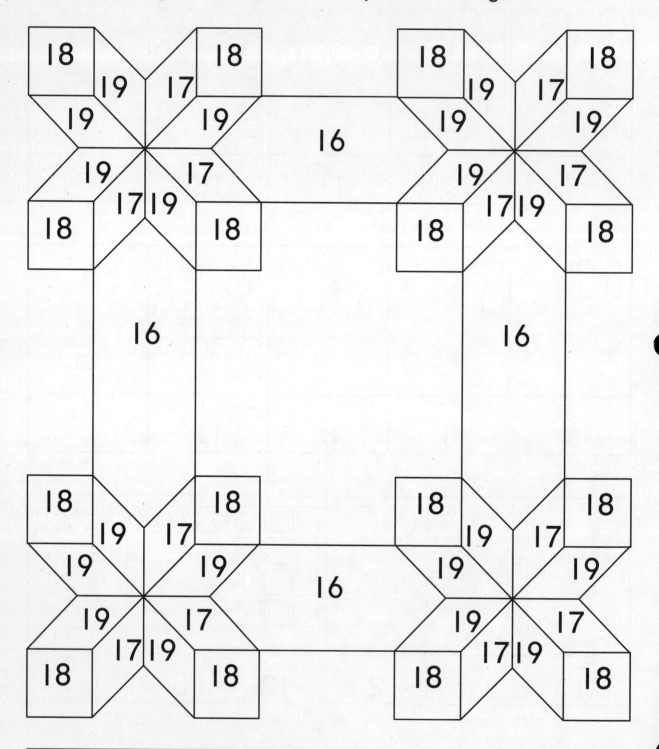

Notes for Home Your child recognized the numerals from 16 to 19 and colored a design according to the numerals in its parts. *Home Activity:* Ask your child to count the number of squares in the design. (16)

Name _____

Decision Making

How long would it take you?

Notes for Home Your child decided how long he or she would spend in various activities (less than 5 minutes, about 10 minutes, more than 15 minutes). *Home Activity:* Ask your child to explain the reasons for his or her choices.

Name _____

Visual Thinking

Follow the dots.

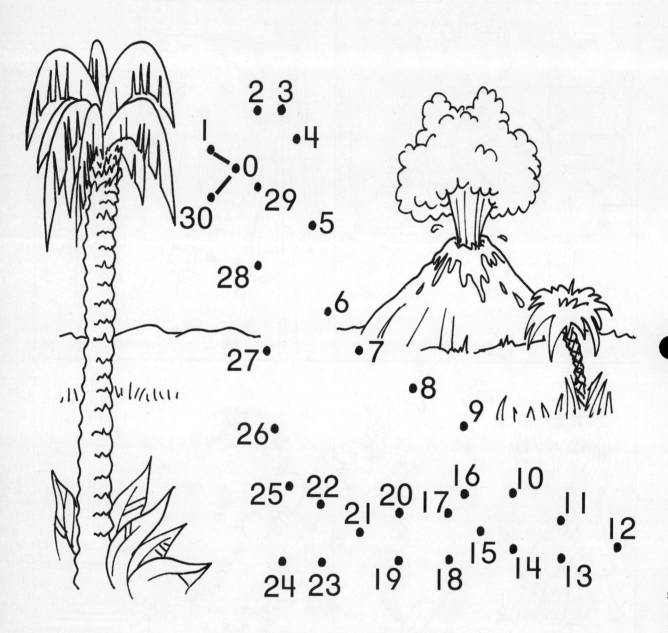

Notes for Home Your child connected the dots in numerical order from 1 through 30. *Home Activity:* Ask your child to count backwards from 30 to 1, following the dots in reverse order.

Decision Making

Complete 1 calendar. Make a picture for it.

FEBRUARY						
S	M	T	W	T	F	S
1	2	3				7
8			11			♡
15		17			20	
	23					28

♡ Valentine's Day

JULY						
S	M	T	W	T	F	S
			1	2		☆
5		7		9		11
12	13	14	15	16	17	18
19				23		25
		29		31		

☆ Independence Day

Notes for Home Your child completed and illustrated a calendar for one month. *Home Activity:* Ask your child to tell you about the holiday celebrated in the month which he or she chose to work with.

Name _____

Visual Thinking

Which group has more?

Circle groups to help you count.

There are more

© Scott Foresman Addison Wesley K

Notes for Home Your child compared the grasshoppers to the butterflies and decided which group has more.
Then he or she circled the correct picture. *Home Activity:* Ask your child to tell you how many butterflies there are
in all. (20)

Name _____

Critical Thinking

Draw lines to match.

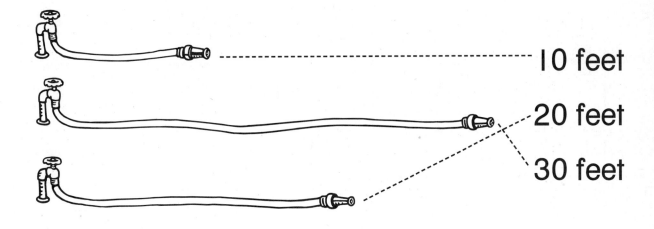

10 feet

20 feet

30 feet

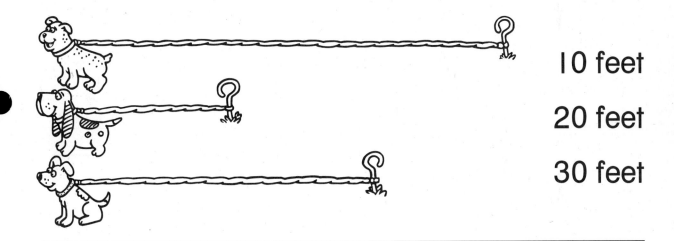

10 feet

20 feet

30 feet

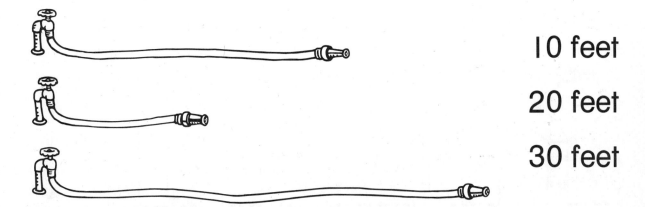

10 feet

20 feet

30 feet

Notes for Home Your child judged the length of each hose and leash and matched it to the appropriate number. *Home Activity:* Ask your child to show you how long he or she thinks 10 feet would be.

© Scott Foresman Addison Wesley K

Name _____

Patterns in Geometry

Show what comes next.

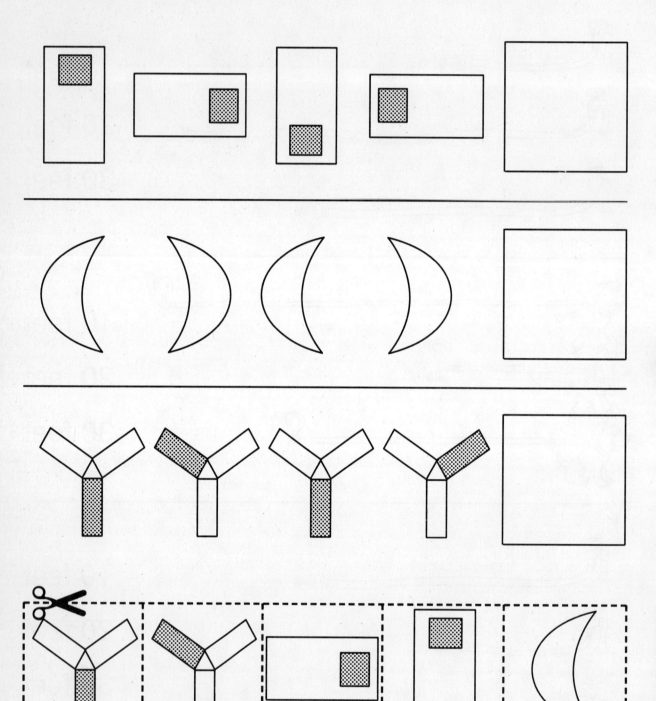

Notes for Home Your child identified the pattern in each row of geometric shapes, and pasted the shape that comes next. *Home Activity:* Ask your child to explain one of the patterns to you.

Name _____

Critical Thinking

Who will make more pairs?

$$\begin{array}{r} 1 \\ + 4 \\ \hline 5 \end{array}$$

$$\begin{array}{r} 2 \\ + 3 \\ \hline 5 \end{array}$$

$$\begin{array}{r} 0 \\ + 5 \\ \hline 5 \end{array}$$

$$\begin{array}{r} 2 \\ + 2 \\ \hline 4 \end{array}$$

$$\begin{array}{r} 5 \\ + 0 \\ \hline 5 \end{array}$$

$$\begin{array}{r} 4 \\ + 1 \\ \hline 5 \end{array}$$

$$\begin{array}{r} 0 \\ + 3 \\ \hline 3 \end{array}$$

$$\begin{array}{r} 3 \\ + 2 \\ \hline 5 \end{array}$$

Andy _____ pairs

$$\begin{array}{r} 3 \\ + 2 \\ \hline 5 \end{array}$$

$$\begin{array}{r} 1 \\ + 2 \\ \hline 3 \end{array}$$

$$\begin{array}{r} 5 \\ + 0 \\ \hline 5 \end{array}$$

$$\begin{array}{r} 4 \\ + 0 \\ \hline 4 \end{array}$$

$$\begin{array}{r} 1 \\ + 4 \\ \hline 5 \end{array}$$

$$\begin{array}{r} 2 \\ + 2 \\ \hline 4 \end{array}$$

$$\begin{array}{r} 0 \\ + 5 \\ \hline 5 \end{array}$$

$$\begin{array}{r} 2 \\ + 3 \\ \hline 5 \end{array}$$

Harris _____ pairs

Notes for Home Your child drew lines to match addition facts to 5 and then circled the child who had the most pairs. *Home Activity:* Ask your child to tell you what cards each player would need to complete 2 more matches.

Patterns

What comes next?

 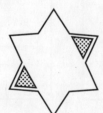  

Notes for Home Your child identified patterns involving the 6 points of a star and drew lines to match each row with the next star in the row. *Home Activity:* Ask your child to explain to you the patterns in rows 3 and 4.

108 Use with pages 283–284.

Decision Making

How many more would you want?

$4 + \underline{6} = \underline{10}$

$2 + \underline{} = \underline{}$

$3 + \underline{} = \underline{}$

Notes for Home Your child drew items that he or she would like more of and wrote an addition fact related to the situation. *Home Activity:* Ask your child to tell a number story about each picture.

Name _____

Visual Thinking

Color only the boxes with the sum of 10.

3 +1	2 +6	5 +5	3 +6	2 +2
5 +3	2 +8	2 +5	3 +7	3 +2
9 +1	7 +1	6 +4	3 +3	1 +9
3 +4	7 +3	3 +5	4 +6	3 +0
0 +4	2 +4	8 +2	1 +6	3 +1

© Scott Foresman Addison Wesley K

Notes for Home Your child colored the boxes with sums of 10. *Home Activity:* Ask your child to find and color the boxes with sums of 4.

Name _____

Critical Thinking

Circle and add.

4 + 2 = 6	3 + 3 = ___
5 + 3 = ___	2 + 6 = ___
5 + 1 = ___	1 + 7 = ___

Notes for Home Your child circled objects to illustrate number sentences and wrote the sum for each sentence. *Home Activity:* Give your child 2 groups of buttons, and have him or her use the buttons to illustrate these number sentences: 3 + 2 (5) and 7 + 3 (10).

Visual Thinking

Do all 3 points match?

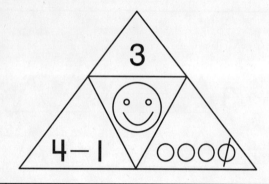 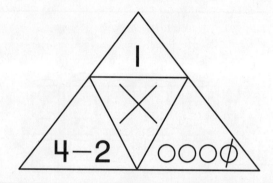

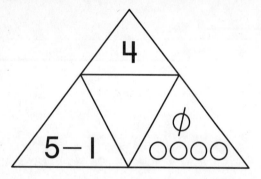 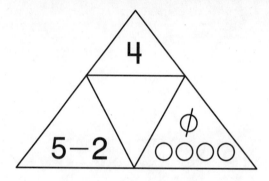

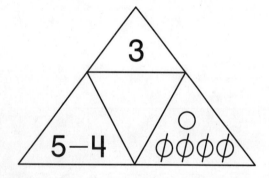 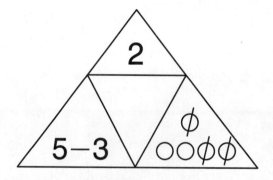

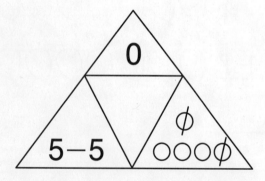 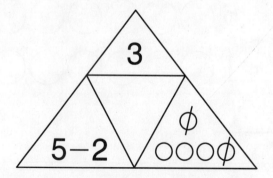

Notes for Home Your child solved each subtraction fact and decided if all the answers in each triangle were the same. If all the answers matched, a happy face was drawn; if the answers didn't match, an X was drawn.
Home Activity: Ask your child to show you how he or she solved a problem.

Decision Making

How many would you give away?

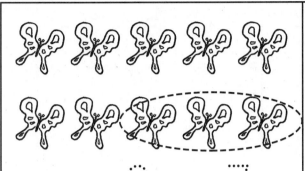

$10 - \underline{3} = \underline{7}$

$9 - \underline{} = \underline{}$

$8 - \underline{} = \underline{}$

$10 - \underline{} = \underline{}$

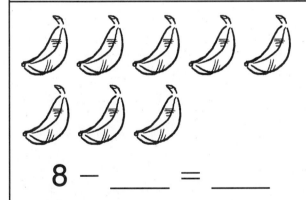

$8 - \underline{} = \underline{}$

$6 - \underline{} = \underline{}$

Notes for Home Your child circled objects he or she would give away and completed subtraction sentences related to that choice. *Home Activity:* Ask your child to draw a picture like one on this page and write a subtraction sentence to go with it.

Name _____

Visual Thinking

Follow the directions and draw a path.

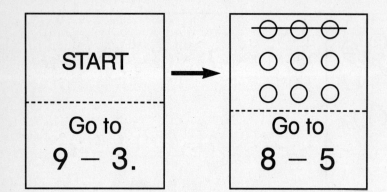

START

Go to
9 − 3.

Go to
8 − 5

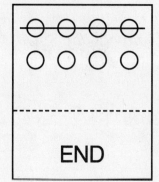

END

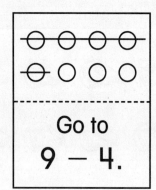

Go to
9 − 4.

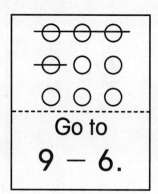

Go to
9 − 6.

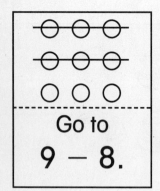

Go to
9 − 8.

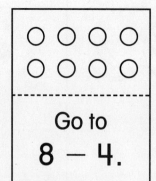

Go to
8 − 4.

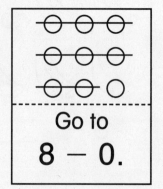

Go to
8 − 0.

Notes for Home Your child matched subtraction facts to pictures representing them, drawing arrows from each box with a fact to the box with the picture of the fact. *Home Activity:* Ask your child to tell an addition fact for one or more of the pictures.

Critical Thinking

Match each monster with the problem it helps solve.

$6 - 3 = \underline{3}$

$4 - 2 = \underline{}$

$8 - 5 = \underline{}$

$5 - 2 = \underline{}$

$2 - 1 = \underline{}$

© Scott Foresman Addison Wesley K

Notes for Home Your child matched monsters with subtraction facts according to the number of arms each monster has. *Home Activity:* Ask your child to draw a picture of a monster with 3 arms and write a subtraction problem using this information.

Name _____

Patterns in Numbers

In each row, do you add (+) or subtract (−)?

					+ or −	
2	5	8	11		___	3
9	8	7	6		___	1
0	3	6	9		___	3
15	13	11	9		___	2
12	10	8	6		___	
2	6	10	14		___	
18	14	10	6		___	

Notes for Home Your child identified the process—addition or subtraction—used in each pattern, and on the last 3 patterns also identified the amount added or subtracted. *Home Activity:* Ask your child to continue each of the addition patterns one more step. (14; 12; 18)

Name _____

Visual Thinking
What do you see?

Notes for Home Your child described what he or she saw in the top, middle, and bottom floor of the apartment building. *Home Activity:* Ask your child to tell you on which floor the cat lives. (The top floor)

Use with pages 3–4. **1**

Name _____

Patterns in Geometry
Draw what comes next.

Notes for Home Your child continued the pattern in each row. *Home Activity:* Ask your child to explain one of the patterns to you.

2 Use with pages 5–6.

Name _____

Critical Thinking
Which does not belong?

Notes for Home Your child put an X on the animal that doesn't belong in each group. *Home Activity:* Ask your child to explain his or her choices.

Use with pages 7–8. **3**

Name _____

Critical Thinking
Match mothers to their babies.

Notes for Home Your child drew lines to match the mother animals to their babies. *Home Activity:* Ask your child to name the animals on the left. (Rabbit, duck, pig, sheep, horse)

4 Use with pages 9–10.

Decision Making

Color the animals that make good pets.

Notes for Home Your child colored the animals that would make good pets. *Home Activity:* Ask your child to explain his or her choices.

Use with pages 11–12. **5**

Patterns in Numbers

Draw what comes next.

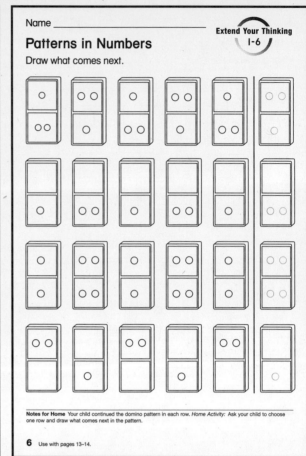

Notes for Home Your child continued the domino pattern in each row. *Home Activity:* Ask your child to choose one row and draw what comes next in the pattern.

6 Use with pages 13–14.

Critical Thinking

Color the things.

green

orange

yellow

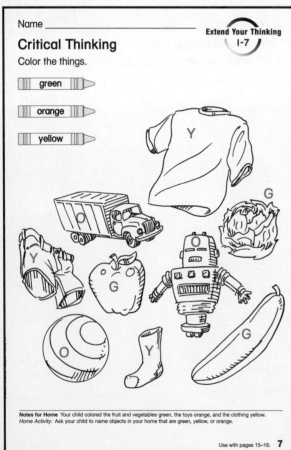

Notes for Home Your child colored the fruit and vegetables green, the toys orange, and the clothing yellow. *Home Activity:* Ask your child to name objects in your home that are green, yellow, or orange.

Use with pages 15–16. **7**

Decision Making

Match each food to the pan that cooked it.

Notes for Home Your child pasted each food to match the pan or tray in which it was cooked. *Home Activity:* Help your child find pans, trays, or other objects in your home that have the same shape as those pictured on the page.

8 Use with pages 17–18.

Visual Thinking

Find Rosa's path home.

She only goes ⇨ , ⇧ , ⇦ , and ⇩ .

Use with pages 19–20. **9**

Critical Thinking

What goes together?

10 Use with pages 27–28.

Visual Thinking

What is missing?

Use with pages 29–30. **11**

Patterns in Numbers

Match the patterns.

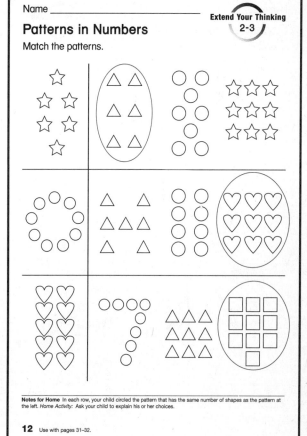

12 Use with pages 31–32.

Name _____

Visual Thinking

Which path takes less time?

2-4Extend Your Thinking
2-4

small**Notes for Home** Your child colored the path that takes less time. *Home Activity:* Ask your child to point to the path that takes more time and explain why. (The path on the right would take more time because it has more curves.)

Use with pages 33–34. **13**

Name _____

Decision Making

What will you pack? Possible answers are given.

Extend Your Thinking
2-5

Notes for Home Your child colored the things she or he would pack for a trip to a beach. *Home Activity:* Ask your child what he or she could do at the beach.

14 Use with pages 35–36.

Name _____

Decision Making

Collect the objects.

Extend Your Thinking
2-6

Notes for Home Your child drew lines to match the objects that each child collects. *Home Activity:* Have your child explain his or her choices. Then ask your child to name one more thing that each child could collect.

Use with pages 37–38. **15**

Name _____

Patterns in Geometry

Find the patterns.

Extend Your Thinking
2-7

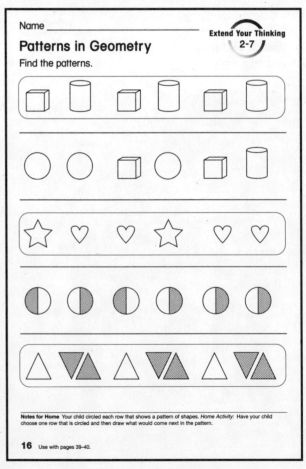

Notes for Home Your child circled each row that shows a pattern of shapes. *Home Activity:* Have your child choose one row that is circled and then draw what would come next in the pattern.

16 Use with pages 39–40.

120

Name _____

Critical Thinking
Make a picture graph.

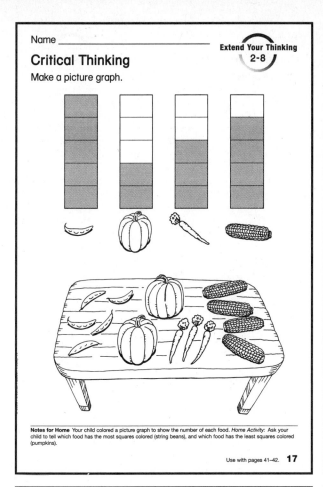

Use with pages 41–42. **17**

Name _____

Extend Your Thinking
2-8

Visual Thinking
What's the musical pattern?

18 Use with pages 49–50.

Extend Your Thinking
3-1

Name _____

Visual Thinking
Which path should each animal take?

Use with pages 51–52. **19**

Extend Your Thinking
3-2

Name _____

Decision Making
Match us to our favorite pets.

Answers may vary.

20 Use with pages 53–54.

Extend Your Thinking
3-3

121

Name _____

Critical Thinking

What happens next?

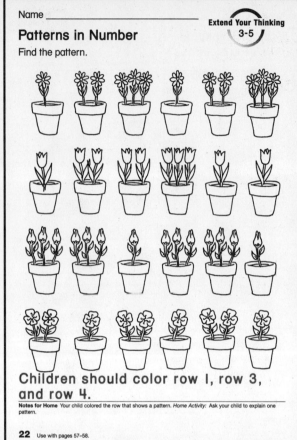

Notes for Home Your child colored the picture that shows what happens next in each row. *Home Activity:* Ask your child to tell what happens first, next and last in each row.

Use with pages 55–56. **21**

Name _____

Patterns in Number

Find the pattern.

Children should color row 1, row 3, and row 4.

Notes for Home Your child colored the row that shows a pattern. *Home Activity:* Ask your child to explain one pattern.

22 Use with pages 57–58.

Name _____

Visual Thinking

What's the pattern?

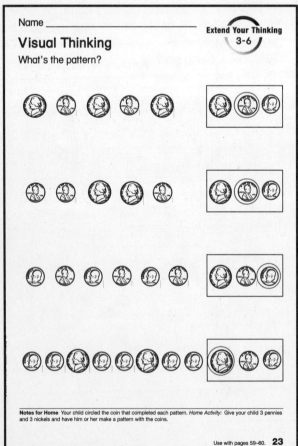

Notes for Home Your child circled the coin that completed each pattern. *Home Activity:* Give your child 3 pennies and 3 nickels and have him or her make a pattern with the coins.

Use with pages 59–60. **23**

Name _____

Decision Making

Plan a party.

Notes for Home Your child used picture clues to color the items needed for a party. *Home Activity:* Ask your child what else she or he would like to have at the party.

24 Use with pages 61–62.

Name _____

Critical Thinking

Match the people to the objects.

Use with pages 69–70. **25**

Name _____

Critical Thinking

Color the things that come in pairs.

26 Use with pages 71–72.

Name _____

Decision Making

Choose what you and 2 friends would eat for breakfast.

Answers will vary, but children should choose enough food for 3 children.

Use with pages 73–74. **27**

Name _____

Critical Thinking

Match the bees to their hives.

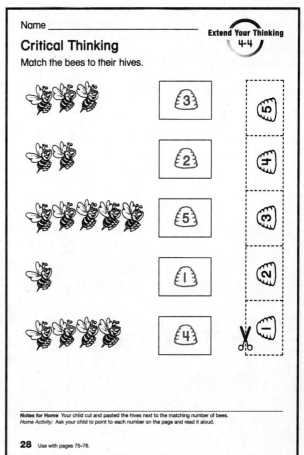

28 Use with pages 75–76.

123

Visual Thinking

Find the patterns using groups of 3 and 4 beads.

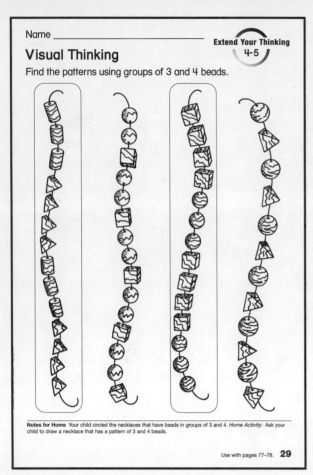

Notes for Home Your child circled the necklaces that have beads in groups of 3 and 4. Home Activity: Ask your child to draw a necklace that has a pattern of 3 and 4 beads.

Use with pages 77–78. **29**

Patterns in Numbers

Draw the petals.

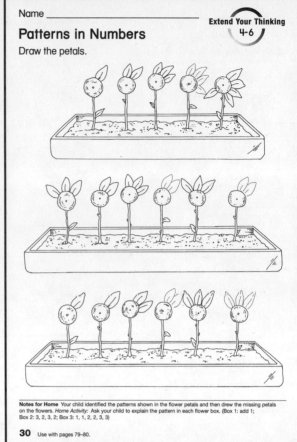

Notes for Home Your child identified the patterns shown in the flower petals and then drew the missing petals on the flowers. Home Activity: Ask your child to explain the pattern in each flower box. (Box 1: add 1; Box 2: 3, 2, 3, 2; Box 3: 1, 1, 2, 2, 3, 3)

30 Use with pages 79–80.

Visual Thinking

How many do you see in each group?

Notes for Home Your child identified groups of 0 to 5 and then recorded the number in the table. Home Activity: Ask your child to tell how many adults there are in the picture (1) and how many water fountains there are in the picture (1).

Use with pages 81–82. **31**

Critical Thinking

How many wheels are there?

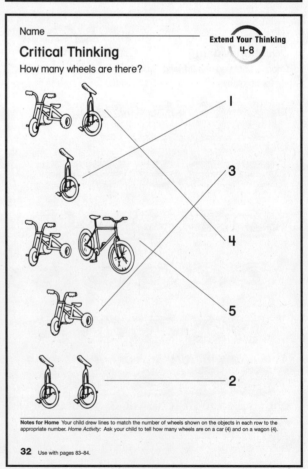

Notes for Home Your child drew lines to match the number of wheels shown on the objects in each row to the appropriate number. Home Activity: Ask your child to tell how many wheels are on a car (4) and on a wagon (4).

32 Use with pages 83–84.

Critical Thinking

Write the numbers.

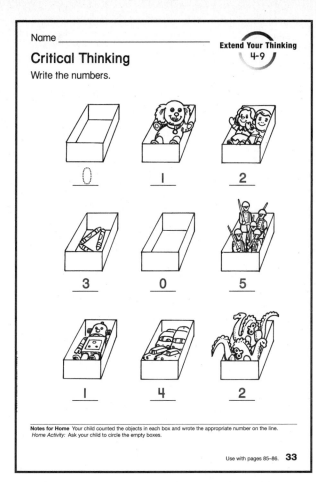

Notes for Home Your child counted the objects in each box and wrote the appropriate number on the line. *Home Activity:* Ask your child to circle the empty boxes.

Use with pages 85–86. **33**

Patterns in Geometry

Draw what comes next in each row.

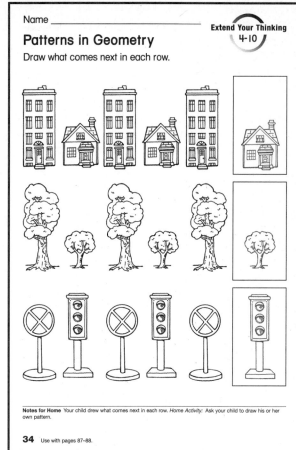

Notes for Home Your child drew what comes next in each row. *Home Activity:* Ask your child to draw his or her own pattern.

34 Use with pages 87–88.

Decision Making

Which will you build?

Answers will vary.

What will you use?

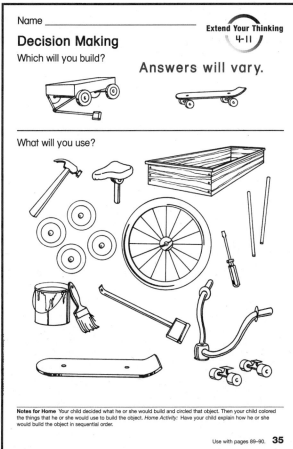

Notes for Home Your child decided what he or she would build and circled that object. Then your child colored the things that he or she would use to build the object. *Home Activity:* Have your child explain how he or she would build the object in sequential order.

Use with pages 89–90. **35**

Visual Thinking

Find the numbers and color.

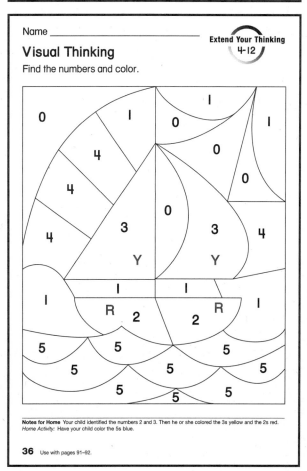

Notes for Home Your child identified the numbers 2 and 3. Then he or she colored the 3s yellow and the 2s red. *Home Activity:* Have your child color the 5s blue.

36 Use with pages 91–92.

Critical Thinking

Circle the object that does not belong.

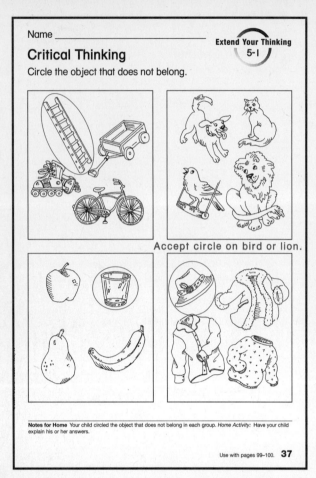

Accept circle on bird or lion.

Notes for Home Your child circled the object that does not belong in each group. Home Activity: Have your child explain his or her answers.

Use with pages 99–100. 37

Visual Thinking

Put the animals in their homes.

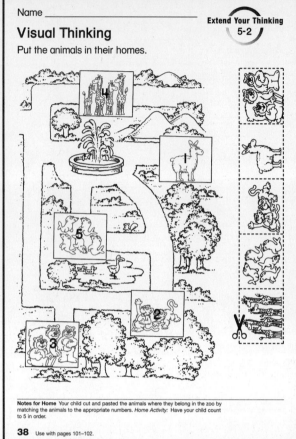

Notes for Home Your child cut and pasted the animals where they belong in the zoo by matching the animals to the appropriate numbers. Home Activity: Have your child count to 5 in order.

38 Use with pages 101–102.

Visual Thinking

Count the objects.

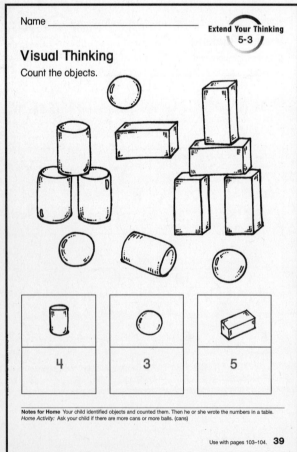

4	3	5

Notes for Home Your child identified objects and counted them. Then he or she wrote the numbers in a table. Home Activity: Ask your child if there are more cans or more balls. (cans)

Use with pages 103–104. 39

Critical Thinking

Match the clowns to dots on their ties.

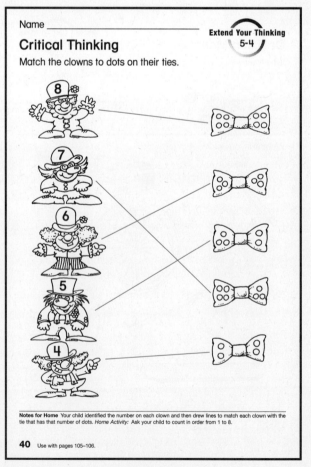

Notes for Home Your child identified the number on each clown and then drew lines to match each clown with the tie that has that number of dots. Home Activity: Ask your child to count in order from 1 to 8.

40 Use with pages 105–106.

Name _____

Patterns in Number

Draw what is missing.

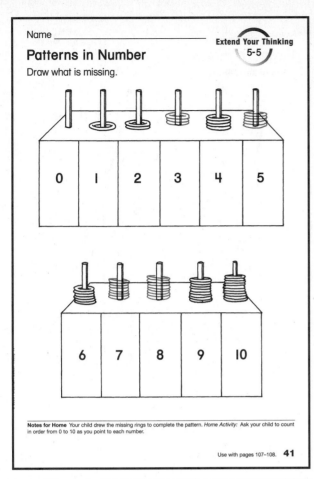

| 0 | 1 | 2 | 3 | 4 | 5 |

| 6 | 7 | 8 | 9 | 10 |

Notes for Home Your child drew the missing rings to complete the pattern. *Home Activity:* Ask your child to count in order from 0 to 10 as you point to each number.

Use with pages 107–108. **41**

Name _____

Critical Thinking

Write the numbers.

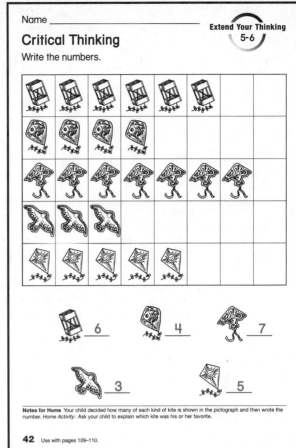

Notes for Home Your child decided how many of each kind of kite is shown in the pictograph and then wrote the number. *Home Activity:* Ask your child to explain which kite was his or her favorite.

42 Use with pages 109–110.

Name _____

Decision Making

Circle 5 toys.

Answers will vary.

Notes for Home Your child chose 5 toys and wrote their numbers in order. *Home Activity:* Ask your child to recite the numbers 1 to 10 in order.

Use with pages 111–112. **43**

Name _____

Visual Thinking

Draw objects.

Check children's drawings.

Notes for Home Your child drew 1 house with 4 windows, 2 trees, 5 birds, and 8 flowers. *Home Activity:* Ask your child to draw 3 bikes in front of the house.

44 Use with pages 113–114.

Critical Thinking

Who is the strongest?

Notes for Home Your child counted the shaded boxes on each scale and wrote the number to tell who was the strongest. Then he or she circled the strongest clown by determining which clown has the most shaded boxes. *Home Activity:* Ask your child to put an X on the weakest clown and explain his or her choice.

Use with pages 115–116. **45**

Extend Your Thinking 5-9

Visual Thinking

Connect the dots.

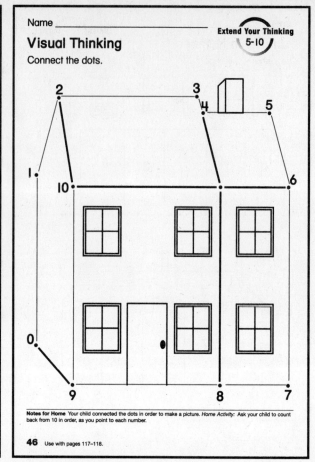

Notes for Home Your child connected the dots in order to make a picture. *Home Activity:* Ask your child to count back from 10 in order, as you point to each number.

46 Use with pages 117–118.

Extend Your Thinking 5-10

Patterns in Geometry

Find the patterns.

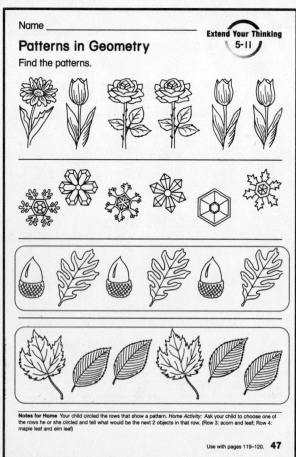

Notes for Home Your child circled the rows that show a pattern. *Home Activity:* Ask your child to choose one of the rows he or she circled and tell what would be the next 2 objects in that row. (Row 3: acorn and leaf; Row 4: maple leaf and elm leaf)

Use with pages 119–120. **47**

Extend Your Thinking 5-11

Decision Making

What would you use?

Notes for Home Your child looked at each scene and then colored the object that would be most useful in that situation. *Home Activity:* Ask your child to name at least one other thing he or she would use in each situation, such as a raincoat on a rainy day.

48 Use with pages 121–122.

Extend Your Thinking 5-12

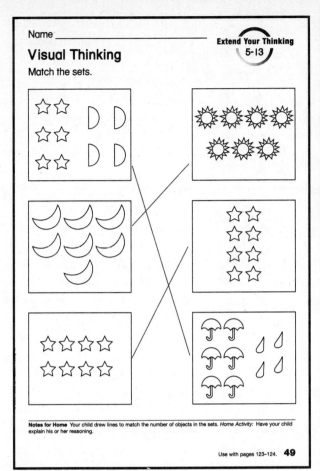

Name _____

Visual Thinking

Match the sets.

Notes for Home Your child drew lines to match the number of objects in the sets. *Home Activity:* Have your child explain his or her reasoning.

Use with pages 123–124. **49**

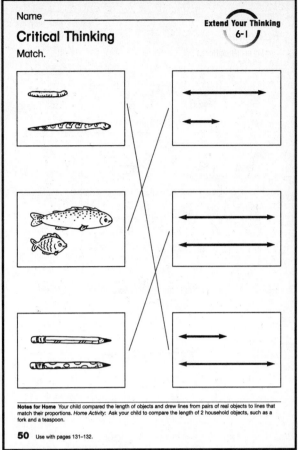

Name _____

Critical Thinking

Match.

Notes for Home Your child compared the length of objects and drew lines from pairs of real objects to lines that match their proportions. *Home Activity:* Ask your child to compare the length of 2 household objects, such as a fork and a teaspoon.

50 Use with pages 131–132.

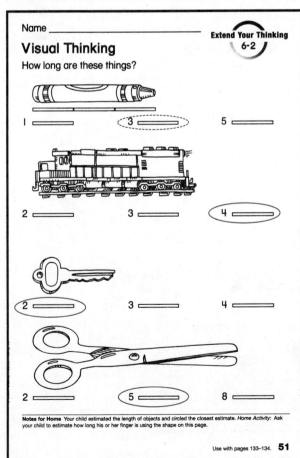

Name _____

Visual Thinking

How long are these things?

Notes for Home Your child estimated the length of objects and circled the closest estimate. *Home Activity:* Ask your child to estimate how long his or her finger is using the shape on this page.

Use with pages 133–134. **51**

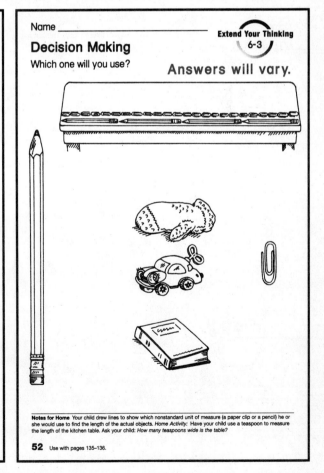

Name _____

Decision Making

Which one will you use?

Answers will vary.

Notes for Home Your child drew lines to show which nonstandard unit of measure (a paper clip or a pencil) he or she would use to find the length of the actual objects. *Home Activity:* Have your child use a teaspoon to measure the length of the kitchen table. Ask your child: *How many teaspoons wide is the table?*

52 Use with pages 135–136.

Name _____

Patterns

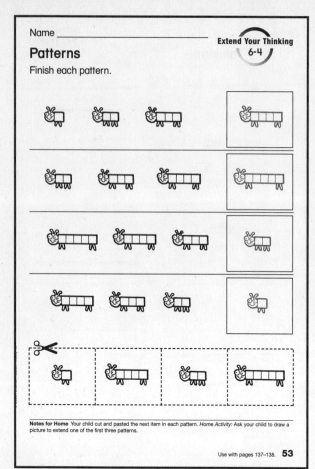

Finish each pattern.

Notes for Home Your child cut and pasted the next item in each pattern. *Home Activity:* Ask your child to draw a picture to extend one of the first three patterns.

Use with pages 137–138. **53**

Name _____

Decision Making

Which one would you use?

Answers will vary.

Notes for Home Your child compared the capacity of different containers and chose the one he or she considered most appropriate for a given task. *Home Activity:* Ask your child to explain his or her reasoning.

54 Use with pages 139–140.

Name _____

Visual Thinking

Draw lines to match.

Notes for Home Your child drew lines connecting soup tureens of different sizes to the groups of small bowls that could be filled from each. *Home Activity:* Ask your child to estimate how many water glasses can be filled from a pitcher and then help him or her test the guess.

Use with pages 141–142. **55**

Name _____

Critical Thinking

Which one is lightest?

Notes for Home Your child compared the weights of objects, circling the object in each row that weighs the least. *Home Activity:* Ask your child to guess which member of your family weighs the least. Then check his or her guess by weighing all family members and comparing their weights.

56 Use with pages 143–144.

Name _____

Visual Thinking

Draw a line to the right group.

heavy

light

Notes for Home Your child estimated the weight of animals and grouped them as heavy or light. *Home Activity:* Ask your child to guess which animal is heavier—a squirrel or an eagle—and then together look up their weights in an encyclopedia to find the answer.

Use with pages 145–146. **57**

Name _____

Patterns

Circle the patterns.

Notes for Home Your child identified and circled patterns involving shapes. *Home Activity:* Ask your child what he or she would change in the second row of shapes to make a pattern. (Possible answer: change the last small square into a large square.)

58 Use with pages 147–148.

Name _____

Visual Thinking

Which are boxes, cylinders, or balls?

Answers will vary.

color

Notes for Home Your child identified rectangular prisms or boxes, cylinders, and spheres or balls. He or she drew an X on each box, colored the cylinders, and circled the spheres. *Home Activity:* Ask your child to draw spots on the cones in the picture.

Use with pages 155–156. **59**

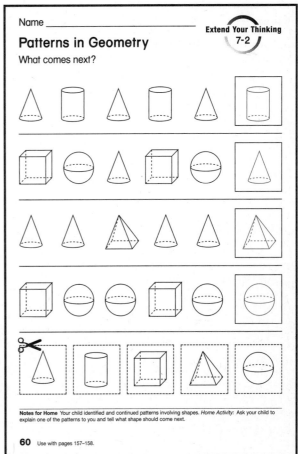

Name _____

Patterns in Geometry

What comes next?

Notes for Home Your child identified and continued patterns involving shapes. *Home Activity:* Ask your child to explain one of the patterns to you and tell what shape should come next.

60 Use with pages 157–158.

Critical Thinking

Which hole will each shape go through?

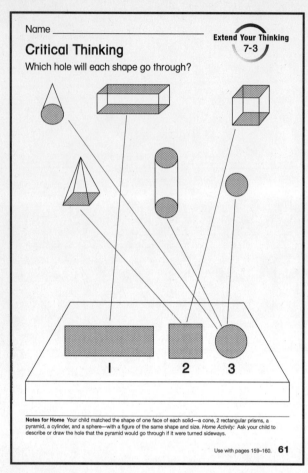

1   2   3

Notes for Home Your child matched the shape of one face of each solid—a cone, 2 rectangular prisms, a pyramid, a cylinder, and a sphere—with a figure of the same shape and size. Home Activity: Ask your child to describe or draw the hole that the pyramid would go through if it were turned sideways.

Use with pages 159–160. **61**

Extend Your Thinking
7-3

Critical Thinking

Which one does not belong?

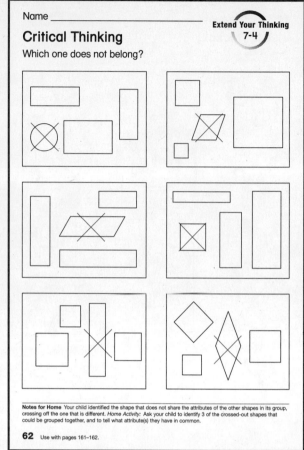

Notes for Home Your child identified the shape that does not share the attributes of the other shapes in its group, crossing off the one that is different. Home Activity: Ask your child to identify 3 of the crossed-out shapes that could be grouped together, and to tell what attribute(s) they have in common.

62 Use with pages 161–162.

Extend Your Thinking
7-4

Patterns in Geometry

Draw what comes next.

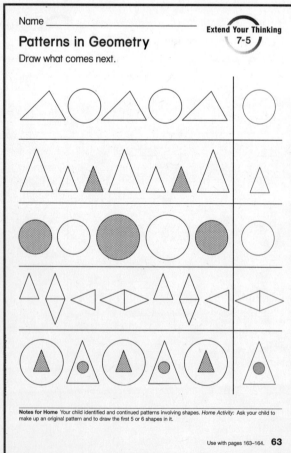

Notes for Home Your child identified and continued patterns involving shapes. Home Activity: Ask your child to make up an original pattern and to draw the first 5 or 6 shapes in it.

Use with pages 163–164. **63**

Extend Your Thinking
7-5

Decision Making

Draw the shapes to make your own pictures.

Answers will vary.

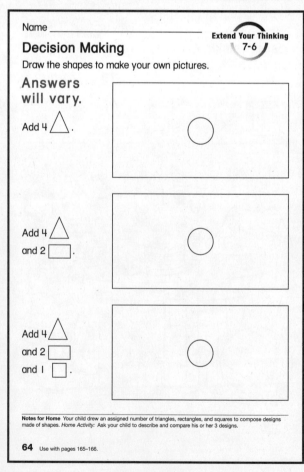

Add 4 △.

Add 4 △ and 2 ▭.

Add 4 △ and 2 ▭ and 1 ▭.

Notes for Home Your child drew an assigned number of triangles, rectangles, and squares to compose designs made of shapes. Home Activity: Ask your child to describe and compare his or her 3 designs.

64 Use with pages 165–166.

Extend Your Thinking
7-6

Visual Thinking

Color the shapes.

Extend Your Thinking
7-7

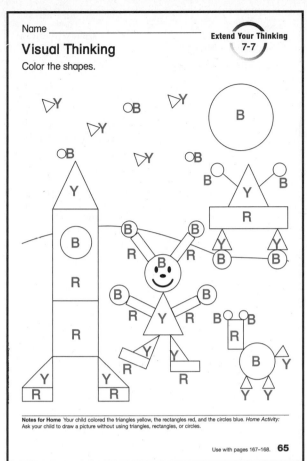

Notes for Home Your child colored the triangles yellow, the rectangles red, and the circles blue. *Home Activity:* Ask your child to draw a picture without using triangles, rectangles, or circles.

Use with pages 167–168. **65**

Patterns

Circle patterns.

Extend Your Thinking
7-8

Notes for Home Your child circled rows with repeating patterns. *Home Activity:* Ask your child to identify the next 3 objects in the pattern in row 4. (fish, turtle, snail)

66 Use with pages 169–170.

Critical Thinking

Draw lines to match.

Extend Your Thinking
7-9

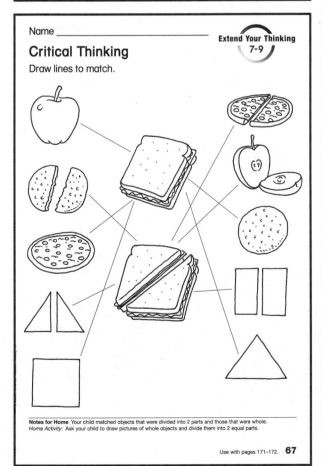

Notes for Home Your child matched objects that were divided into 2 parts and those that were whole. *Home Activity:* Ask your child to draw pictures of whole objects and divide them into 2 equal parts.

Use with pages 171–172. **67**

Decision Making

Draw lines to share.

Extend Your Thinking
7-10

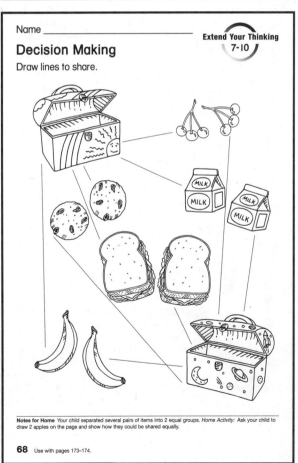

Notes for Home Your child separated several pairs of items into 2 equal groups. *Home Activity:* Ask your child to draw 2 apples on the page and show how they could be shared equally.

68 Use with pages 173–174.

Name _____

Visual Thinking

Color the triangles.

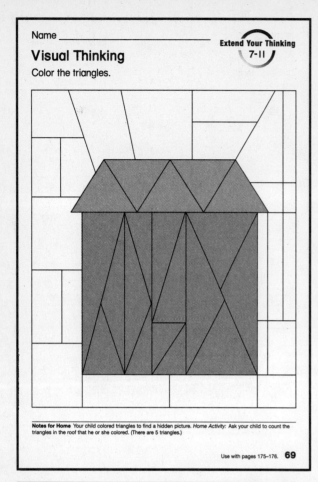

Notes for Home Your child colored triangles to find a hidden picture. Home Activity: Ask your child to count the
triangles in the roof that he or she colored. (There are 5 triangles.)

Use with pages 175–176. **69**

Name _____

Decision Making

Choose a fruit for each box. Draw the right number.

3

5

**Selection of fruits will
vary, but the correct
number should be
drawn in each box.**

7

Notes for Home Your child chose fruits and drew them the correct number of times to illustrate 3 numbers.
Home Activity: Ask your child to choose a fruit and draw it enough times to illustrate the number 4.

70 Use with pages 183–184.

Name _____

Visual Thinking

Trace the path marked by groups of 4 birds.

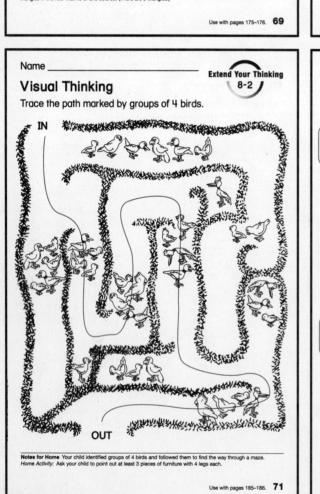

Notes for Home Your child identified groups of 4 birds and followed them to find the way through a maze.
Home Activity: Ask your child to point out at least 3 pieces of furniture with 4 legs each.

Use with pages 185–186. **71**

Name _____

Critical Thinking

Circle each tile with 6 dots in all.

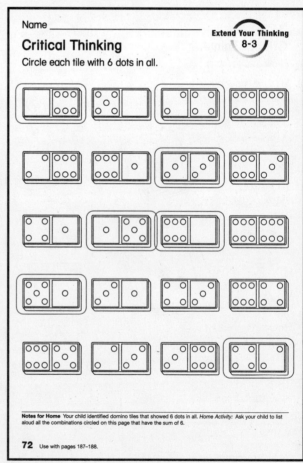

Notes for Home Your child identified domino tiles that showed 6 dots in all. Home Activity: Ask your child to list
aloud all the combinations circled on this page that have the sum of 6.

72 Use with pages 187–188.

Patterns

Name _____

Name _____

Patterns

Name _____

Patterns

What comes next?

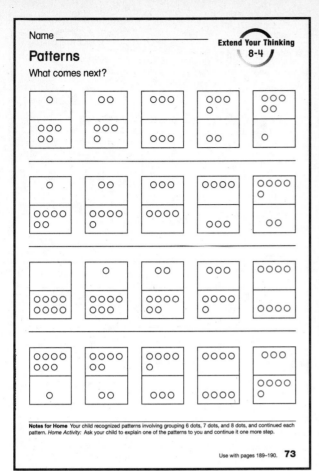

Extend Your Thinking
8-4

Notes for Home Your child recognized patterns involving grouping 6 dots, 7 dots, and 8 dots, and continued each pattern. *Home Activity:* Ask your child to explain one of the patterns to you and continue it one more step.

Use with pages 189–190. **73**

Name _____

Visual Thinking

Connect each pair of groups that make 10.

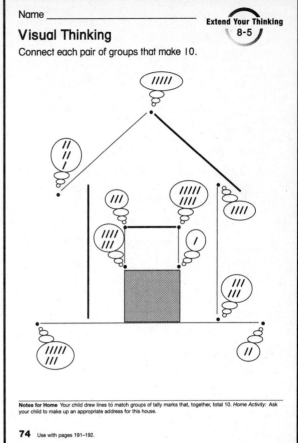

Extend Your Thinking
8-5

Notes for Home Your child drew lines to match groups of tally marks that, together, total 10. *Home Activity:* Ask your child to make up an appropriate address for this house.

74 Use with pages 191–192.

Name _____

Critical Thinking

Count and match.

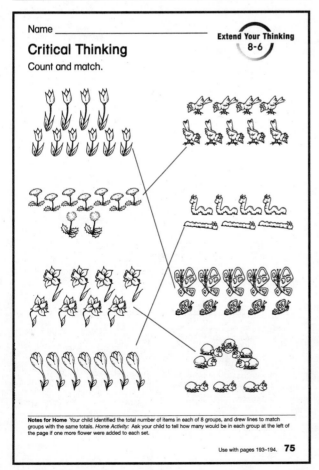

Extend Your Thinking
8-6

Notes for Home Your child identified the total number of items in each of 8 groups, and drew lines to match groups with the same totals. *Home Activity:* Ask your child to tell how many would be in each group at the left of the page if one more flower were added to each set.

Use with pages 193–194. **75**

Name _____

Decision Making

Match each box with any number.
Color that many.

Answers will vary.

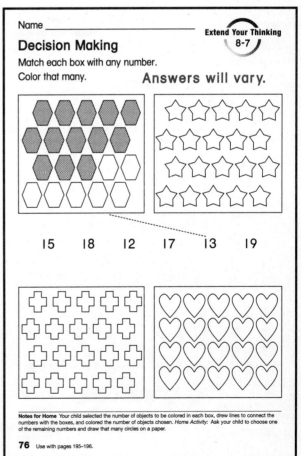

Extend Your Thinking
8-7

15   18   12   17   13   19

Notes for Home Your child selected the number of objects to be colored in each box, drew lines to connect the numbers with the boxes, and colored the number of objects chosen. *Home Activity:* Ask your child to choose one of the remaining numbers and draw that many circles on a paper.

76 Use with pages 195–196.

135

Name _____

Critical Thinking

How much does each weigh?

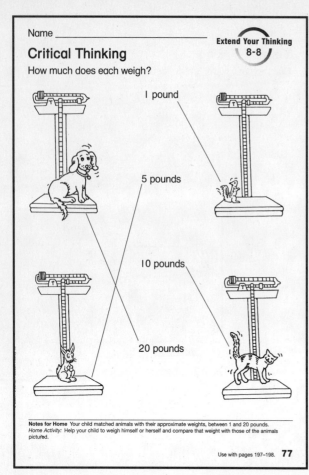

1 pound

5 pounds

10 pounds

20 pounds

Notes for Home Your child matched animals with their approximate weights, between 1 and 20 pounds. *Home Activity:* Help your child to weigh himself or herself and compare that weight with those of the animals pictured.

Use with pages 197–198. **77**

Name _____

Visual Thinking

How long is each thing?

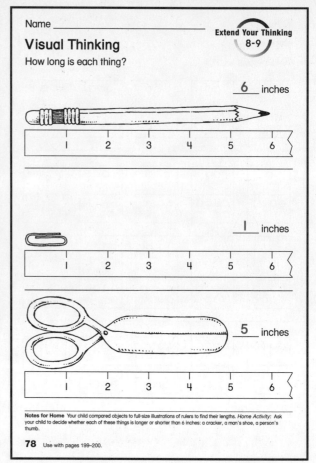

_6_ inches

_1_ inches

_5_ inches

Notes for Home Your child compared objects to full-size illustrations of rulers to find their lengths. *Home Activity:* Ask your child to decide whether each of these things is longer or shorter than 6 inches: a cracker, a man's shoe, a person's thumb.

78 Use with pages 199–200.

Name _____

Patterns

What comes next?

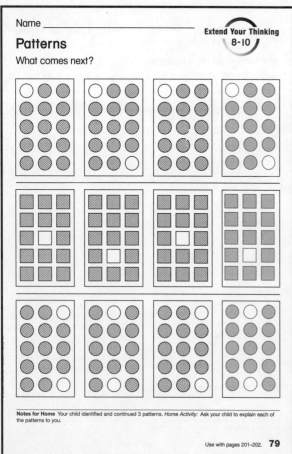

Notes for Home Your child identified and continued 3 patterns. *Home Activity:* Ask your child to explain each of the patterns to you.

Use with pages 201–202. **79**

Name _____

Critical Thinking

What comes before or after?

Notes for Home Your child identified events that come before and after given events. *Home Activity:* Ask your child to explain what is happening in each of the pictures.

80 Use with pages 209–210.

Patterns

What comes next?

Notes for Home Your child identified the next event in a repeating pattern of events. *Home Activity:* Ask your child to dramatize one of the exercises pictured on this page.

Use with pages 211–212. **81**

Visual Thinking

Cross out the clocks that are wrong.

Notes for Home Your child identified clocks whose numerals were incorrect or missing. *Home Activity:* Ask your child to explain what was wrong with each of the clocks he or she crossed out.

82 Use with pages 213–214.

Decision Making

What time would you do this?

Answers will vary.

Notes for Home Your child read clocks to the hour and circled preferred times for given activities. *Home Activity:* Ask your child to explain his or her choices.

Use with pages 215–216. **83**

Critical Thinking

What comes before the party?

Notes for Home Your child circled events that usually happen before a birthday party. *Home Activity:* Ask your child to think of events that happen during and after a birthday party.

84 Use with pages 217–218.

Name _____

Visual Thinking

Draw a line to find the pennies.

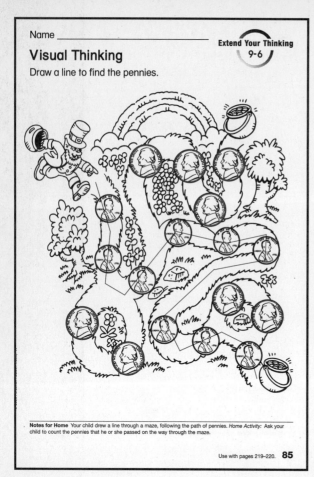

Notes for Home Your child drew a line through a maze, following the path of pennies. **Home Activity:** Ask your child to count the pennies that he or she passed on the way through the maze.

Use with pages 219–220. **85**

Name _____

Decision Making

Choose 2 things to buy with

these coins:

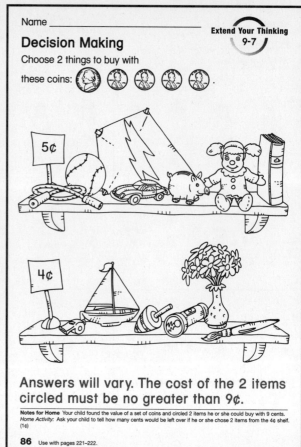

Answers will vary. The cost of the 2 items circled must be no greater than 9¢.

Notes for Home Your child found the value of a set of coins and circled 2 items he or she could buy with 9 cents. *Home Activity:* Ask your child to tell how many cents would be left over if he or she chose 2 items from the 4¢ shelf. (1¢)

86 Use with pages 221–222.

Name _____

Patterns

What comes next?

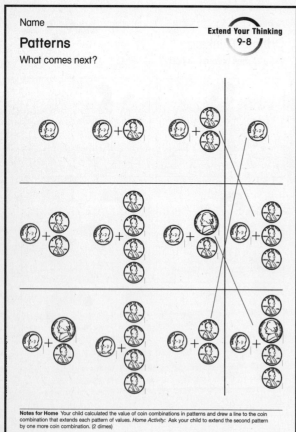

Notes for Home Your child calculated the value of coin combinations in patterns and drew a line to the coin combination that extends each pattern of values. **Home Activity:** Ask your child to extend the second pattern by one more coin combination. (2 dimes)

Use with pages 223–224. **87**

Name _____

Critical Thinking

Which ones can I buy?

Notes for Home Your child decided the value of a coin combination and circled items that cost that amount or less. **Home Activity:** Ask your child to choose one thing he or she would buy with the given amount of money and the same choices of items.

88 Use with pages 225–226.

Name _____

Visual Thinking

Cross out the gift that is wrong for each one.

Notes for Home Your child crossed out the gift that was not appropriate. *Home Activity:* Ask your child to explain his or her choices.

Use with pages 227–228. **89**

Name _____

Visual Thinking

Circle how many are coming.

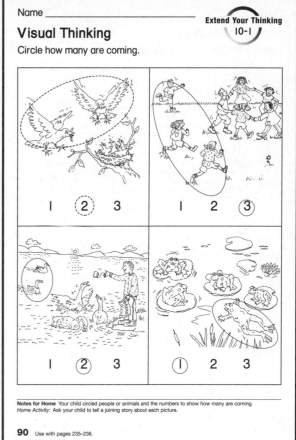

Notes for Home Your child circled people or animals and the numbers to show how many are coming. *Home Activity:* Ask your child to tell a joining story about each picture.

90 Use with pages 235–236.

Name _____

Decision Making

Draw how many you want.

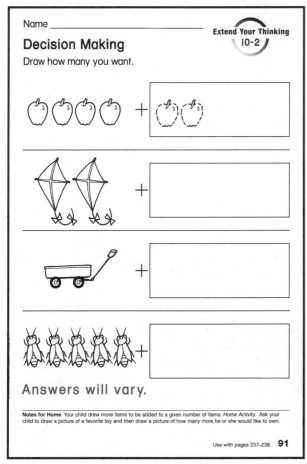

Answers will vary.

Notes for Home Your child drew more items to be added to a given number of items. *Home Activity:* Ask your child to draw a picture of a favorite toy and then draw a picture of how many more he or she would like to own.

Use with pages 237–238. **91**

Name _____

Critical Thinking

Circle how many are left.

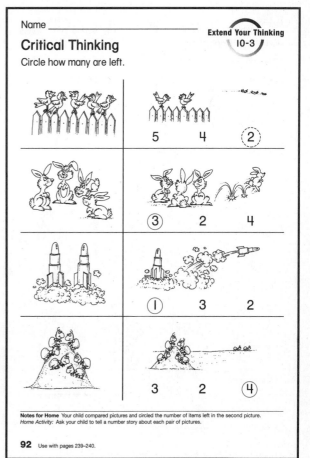

Notes for Home Your child compared pictures and circled the number of items left in the second picture. *Home Activity:* Ask your child to tell a number story about each pair of pictures.

92 Use with pages 239–240.

Name _____

Decision Making

How much goes to the first animal?

Extend Your Thinking 10-4

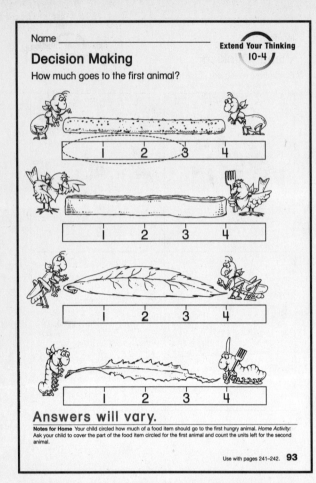

Answers will vary.

Notes for Home Your child circled how much of a food item should go to the first hungry animal. *Home Activity:* Ask your child to cover the part of the food item circled for the first animal and count the units left for the second animal.

Use with pages 241–242. **93**

Name _____

Patterns in Numbers

Circle the number that is missing.

Extend Your Thinking 10-5

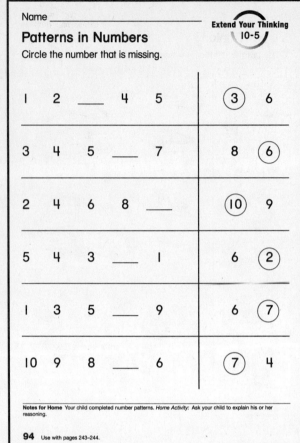

Notes for Home Your child completed number patterns. *Home Activity:* Ask your child to explain his or her reasoning.

94 Use with pages 243–244.

Name _____

Critical Thinking

Cross off the ones that are not equal.

Extend Your Thinking 10-6

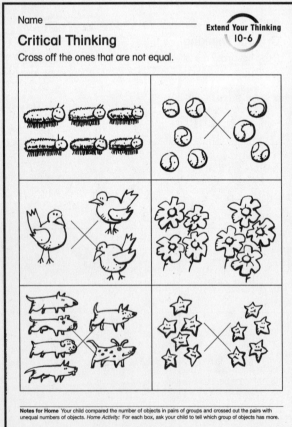

Notes for Home Your child compared the number of objects in pairs of groups and crossed out the pairs with unequal numbers of objects. *Home Activity:* For each box, ask your child to tell which group of objects has more.

Use with pages 245–246. **95**

Name _____

Visual Thinking

Circle the longer object.

Extend Your Thinking 10-7

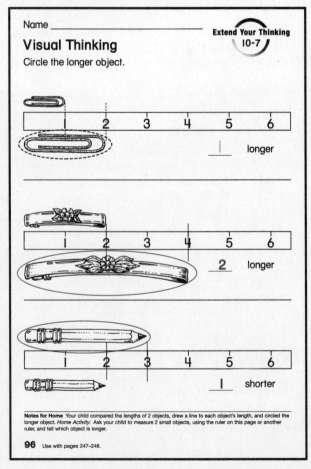

Notes for Home Your child compared the lengths of 2 objects, drew a line to each object's length, and circled the longer object. *Home Activity:* Ask your child to measure 2 small objects, using the ruler on this page or another ruler, and tell which object is longer.

96 Use with pages 247–248.

140

Name _____

Patterns

What comes next?

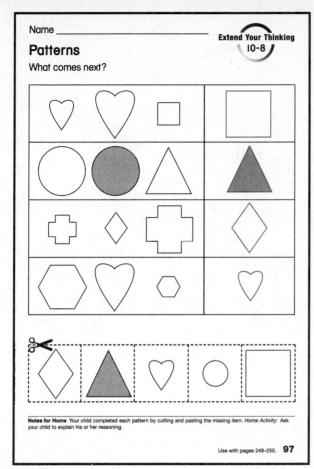

Notes for Home Your child completed each pattern by cutting and pasting the missing item. *Home Activity:* Ask your child to explain his or her reasoning.

Name _____

Critical Thinking

Count. Circle the correct numbers.

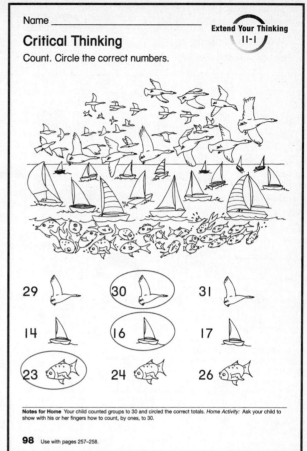

29   30   31

14   16   17

23   24   26

Notes for Home Your child counted groups to 30 and circled the correct totals. *Home Activity:* Ask your child to show with his or her fingers how to count, by ones, to 30.

Name _____

Patterns in Numbers

What comes next?

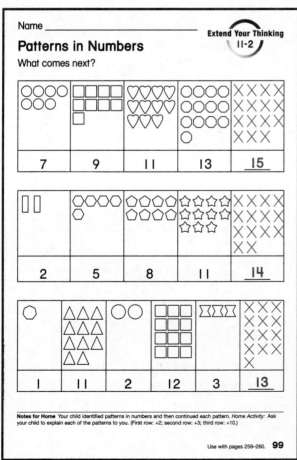

| 7 | 9 | 11 | 13 | 15 |

| 2 | 5 | 8 | 11 | 14 |

| 1 | 11 | 2 | 12 | 3 | 13 |

Notes for Home Your child identified patterns in numbers and then continued each pattern. *Home Activity:* Ask your child to explain each of the patterns to you. (First row: +2; second row: +3; third row: +10.)

Name _____

Visual Thinking

Color by numbers.
16—orange   17—blue   18—yellow   19—green

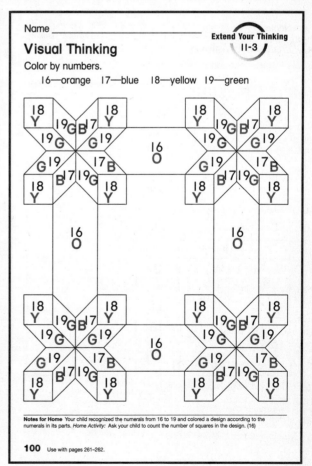

Notes for Home Your child recognized the numerals from 16 to 19 and colored a design according to the numerals in its parts. *Home Activity:* Ask your child to count the number of squares in the design. (16)

Name _____

Decision Making

How long would it take you?   **Answers will vary.**

Notes for Home Your child decided how long he or she would spend in various activities (less than 5 minutes, about 10 minutes, more than 15 minutes). *Home Activity:* Ask your child to explain the reasons for his or her choices.

Use with pages 263–264.   **101**

Name _____

Visual Thinking

Follow the dots.

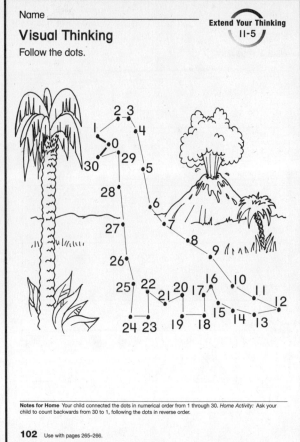

Notes for Home Your child connected the dots in numerical order from 1 through 30. *Home Activity:* Ask your child to count backwards from 30 to 1, following the dots in reverse order.

102   Use with pages 265–266.

Name _____

Decision Making

Complete 1 calendar. Make a picture for it.

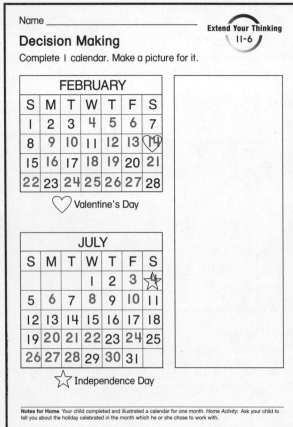

Notes for Home Your child completed and illustrated a calendar for one month. *Home Activity:* Ask your child to tell you about the holiday celebrated in the month which he or she chose to work with.

Use with pages 267–266.   **103**

Name _____

Visual Thinking

Which group has more?

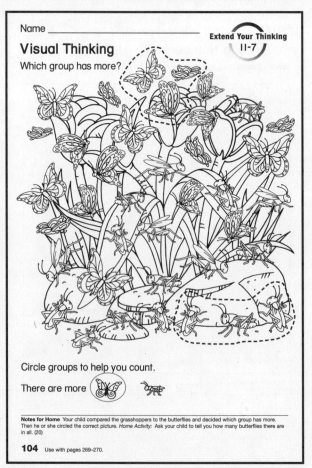

Circle groups to help you count.

There are more 🦋 🦗

Notes for Home Your child compared the grasshoppers to the butterflies and decided which group has more. Then he or she circled the correct picture. *Home Activity:* Ask your child to tell you how many butterflies there are in all. (20)

104   Use with pages 269–270.

Critical Thinking

Draw lines to match.

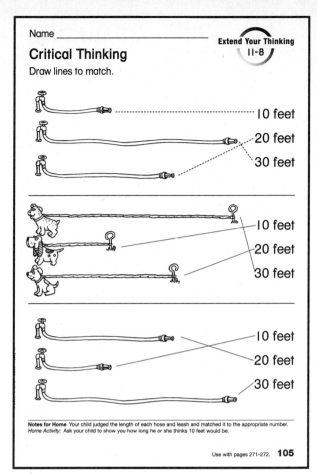

Notes for Home Your child judged the length of each hose and leash and matched it to the appropriate number.
Home Activity: Ask your child to show you how long he or she thinks 10 feet would be.

Use with pages 271–272. **105**

Patterns in Geometry

Show what comes next.

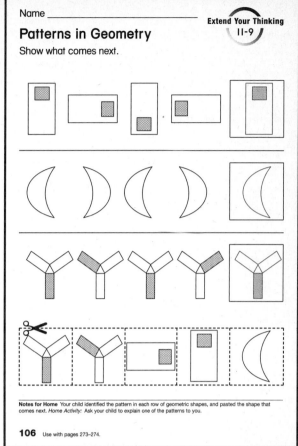

Notes for Home Your child identified the pattern in each row of geometric shapes, and pasted the shape that
comes next. Home Activity: Ask your child to explain one of the patterns to you.

106 Use with pages 273–274.

Critical Thinking

Who will make more pairs?

Andy _____3_____ pairs

Harris _____2_____ pairs

Notes for Home Your child drew lines to match addition facts to 5 and then circled the child who had the most
pairs. Home Activity: Ask your child to tell you what cards each player would need to complete 2 more matches.

Use with pages 281–282. **107**

Patterns

What comes next?

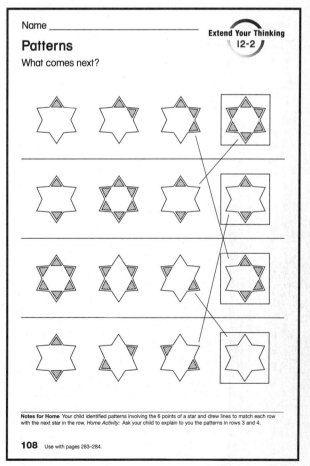

Notes for Home Your child identified patterns involving the 6 points of a star and drew lines to match each row
with the next star in the row. Home Activity: Ask your child to explain to you the patterns in rows 3 and 4.

108 Use with pages 283–284.

143

Decision Making

How many more would you want?

Answers will vary.

$4 + \underline{6} = \underline{10}$

 +

$2 + \underline{} = \underline{}$

+

$3 + \underline{} = \underline{}$

Visual Thinking

Color only the boxes with the sum of 10.

3 $+1$	2 $+6$	5 $+5$	3 $+6$	2 $+2$
5 $+3$	2 $+8$	2 $+5$	3 $+7$	3 $+2$
9 $+1$	7 $+1$	6 $+4$	3 $+3$	1 $+9$
3 $+4$	7 $+3$	3 $+5$	4 $+6$	3 $+0$
0 $+4$	2 $+4$	8 $+2$	1 $+6$	3 $+1$

Critical Thinking

Circle and add.

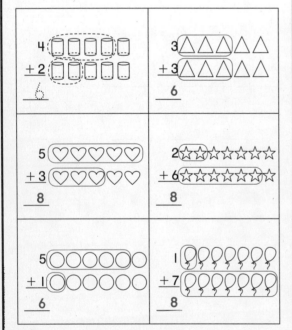

Visual Thinking

Do all 3 points match?

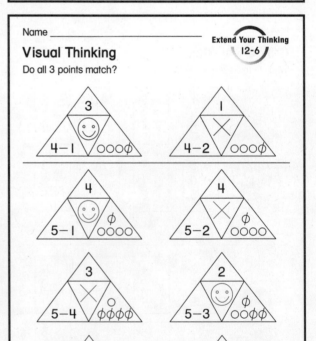

Decision Making

How many would you give away? **Answers will vary.**

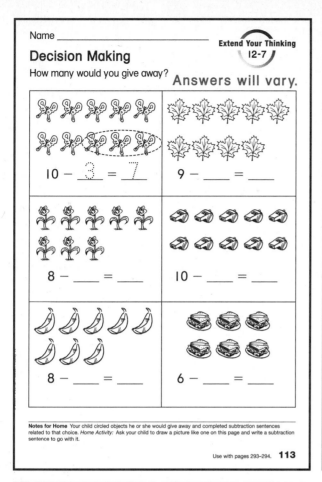

$10 - 3 = 7$

$9 - \_\_\_ = \_\_\_$

$8 - \_\_\_ = \_\_\_$

$10 - \_\_\_ = \_\_\_$

$8 - \_\_\_ = \_\_\_$

$6 - \_\_\_ = \_\_\_$

Visual Thinking

Follow the directions and draw a path.

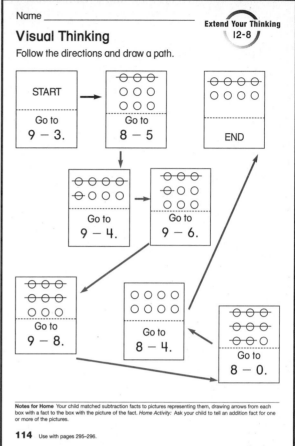

START

Go to $9 - 3$.

Go to $8 - 5$.

END

Go to $9 - 4$.

Go to $9 - 6$.

Go to $9 - 8$.

Go to $8 - 4$.

Go to $8 - 0$.

Critical Thinking

Match each monster with the problem it helps solve.

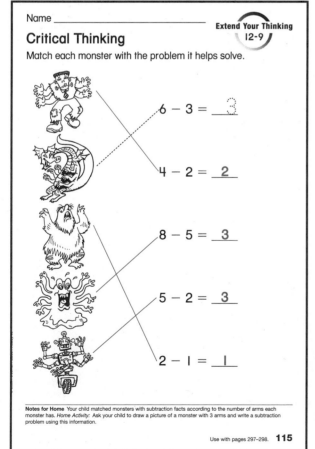

$6 - 3 = 3$

$4 - 2 = 2$

$8 - 5 = 3$

$5 - 2 = 3$

$2 - 1 = 1$

Patterns in Numbers

In each row, do you add (+) or subtract (−)?

				+ or −	
2	5	8	11	+	3
9	8	7	6	−	1
0	3	6	9	+	3
15	13	11	9	−	2
12	10	8	6	−	2
2	6	10	14	+	4
18	14	10	6	−	4

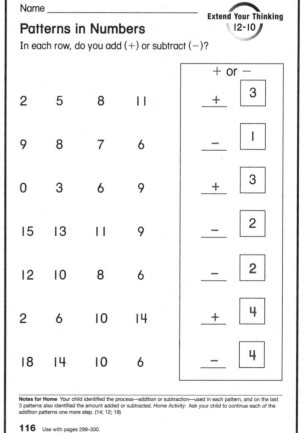